S0-ECR-269

SURVIVING DIVORCE
Men Beyond Marriage

HQ
756
A49
1983

SURVIVING DIVORCE
Men Beyond Marriage

Peter Ambrose
*School of Cultural and Community Studies,
University of Sussex*

John Harper
*Staff Development Officer,
Probation Service*

Richard Pemberton
*Senior Clinical Psychologist,
Victoria Hospital, Lewes*

ROWMAN & ALLANHELD
Totowa, New Jersey

ROWMAN & ALLANHELD

Published in the United States of America in 1983
by Rowman & Allanheld
(A division of Littlefield, Adams & Company)
81 Adams Drive, Totowa, New Jersey 07512

Copyright © 1983 by Peter Ambrose, John Harper,
and Richard Pemberton

All rights reserved. No part of this publication may
be reproduced, stored in a retrieval system, or
transmitted in any form or by any means, electronic,
mechanical, photocopying, recording, or otherwise,
without the prior permission of the publisher.

Library of Congress Cataloging in Publication Data

Ambrose, Peter J.
  Surviving divorce

  1. Divorced fathers—Great Britain.   2. Divorce—
Great Britain.   3. Custody of children—Great
Britain.   I. Harper, John.   II. Pemberton, Richard.
III. Title.
HQ756.A49   1983   306.8′9   82-22717
ISBN 0-86598-122-1

83 84 85/ 10 9 8 7 6 5 4 3 2 1

Printed in Great Britain

For Liz, Linda and all the children

Some Christian teaching on marriage and divorce:

> As God hath ordained remedies for every disease, so He hath ordained a remedie for the disease of marriage. The disease of marriage is adulterie, and the medicine thereof is divorcement . . . thus, He which made marriage did not make it inseperable, for then marriage would be a servitude.
>
> Henry Smith, *Preparative to Marriage*, 1591

> . . . the only argument for more divorce really is the hardship of indissoluble marriage, but this is not argument for it assumes a right of happiness. There is no such right. . . . The path of virtue may often lead to unspeakable misery. . . . The Christian must endure as his Lord endured.
>
> Lord Cecil, Parliamentary Debate, 1937

Contents

Acknowledgements

We would like to record our thanks to the ninety-two men who took the time to complete our survey form and especially to those we interviewed. We hope they will all feel that the result is worthwhile.

Thanks are also due for their friendly co-operation to members of the Probation Service, notably John King of East Sussex and David Huxtable of West Sussex. We were helped in the analysis of the survey by Anna Beckwith, Sheila Kay, Sue Parry and Judie Wadhams and the computer processing of the data was carried out very efficiently by Amanda Dennis of the Research Support Unit at the University of Sussex. The typing was done by Pam Botha and Ann Watson and the final typescript prepared by Sylvia Burton who produced order out of the chaos that results when authors edit each other's work with microscopic inter-linings.

Finally, in an area that has some of the characteristics of a mine-field, the authors wish to make it clear that they alone are responsible for any errors of fact and for the various opinions expressed.

Preface

A few words on the organisation of the book may be helpful. One of the aims has been to write a book that goes beyond the straight reporting of a research project about the ways men experience divorce. We feel it is important to place our findings in as broad a historical, social, political, and legal context as space allows. Since every divorce represents the failure of a marriage, we took it as a crucially important part of our task to spend some time considering the institution of marriage and especially the *expectations* that might reasonably be held by those embarking upon it. This raises complex issues such as the extent to which the aims and codes of behaviour to be observed within marriage are externally defined in some way (and if so who or what defines them) or whether marriage is what every couple chooses to make it. Given that the institution is so central to the structure of most societies, one might have expected a fair degree of agreement about this first and most basic question. On closer examination there appears to be no such agreement.

The opening two chapters of the book are therefore about marriage. The first sketches some aspects of Christian teaching on marriage and divorce and shows how this has been translated into secular codes of law in various historical eras. It deals too with the writings of certain sociologists who clearly (although rarely explicitly) subscribe to a traditional Christian ethic about marriage. The next chapter outlines some critically different concepts of marriage, referring to work by Engels, some radical psychoanalysts, the women's movement, and the views of Laing and some of his associates. These two chapters, taken together, make it clear that almost every important issue surrounding marriage and divorce is, and has been for a long time, hotly contested. Virtually no view is universally accepted. *Yet millions of marriages are contracted as if the issues were unproblematic, the expected codes of behaviour obvious to everybody*. We see in this central paradox a clear clue to the vast amount of bewilderment, disillusion, sadness and stress uncovered in the findings of our research project.

Chapter 3 gives some basic information about the number of

marriage breakdowns and deals especially with the rapid growth in divorce since the changes in matrimonial law which became effective in 1971. Chapter 4 is the first of the chapters dealing with the divorce experiences of the ninety-two men we questioned in our survey. It deals with the divorce itself, who petitioned, on what grounds and the extent to which both the divorce proceedings, and the custody of any children, were contested. In the following chapter we discuss the people, and the agencies, to whom the ninety-two men turned for help and support, and the extent to which these sources were actually successful in affording assistance of various kinds. In view of the special significance of the solicitor as a source of legal, and sometimes other, assistance, Chapter 6 is devoted to an assessment of the service given by the legal profession and the opinions formed of this service by the men in our sample.

Chapter 7 deals with the impact of the divorce on the lives of the men concerned. Following a brief discussion of the general issue of loss and change, separate sections of the chapter deal with changes in mental health, in the role of the divorced man as a father, in his career prospects and financial position and finally with the effects of the divorce on friendship networks and on relationships with parents and in-laws. Chapter 8 seeks to show how the experience of a divorce had led the men in our sample to reassess themselves and to change their attitude towards women, remarriage and the state of matrimonial law. Chapter 9 reviews the current state of the legal debate concerning matrimonial issues and, on the basis of the research findings, offers some suggestions in relation both to possible changes in the law and to non-legislative change that might be carried out to make existing systems of welfare and support more sensitive to the needs of divorced men. Although the discussion is based primarily on English and Scottish law, the issues it covers (such as the extent to which marital conduct should determine financial settlements, and the position of second wives) require consideration in all systems of divorce law.

Our final section, 'Afterthoughts', sums up what we feel we learned from writing the book. We regard this brief discussion of how alternative approaches to marriage might be developed in the future as very important and we urge those who may have jumped a chapter here and there to rejoin us for it. In this section, and elsewhere in the book, we have attempted to consider what might lie 'beyond marriage' not only for the individual but also for society at large.

Chapter 1
Marriage—Some Traditional Views

Reaction to the breakdown of a marriage is bound to depend, to some extent, on the two partners' particular conception of what the institution of marriage is all about. The common use of the word 'breakdown' indicates that, in society's eyes, some fundamental malfunction has occurred, some blame is to be attached and some repair work may be necessary on the people involved. Thus various judicial and welfare branches of the state will begin to operate and, in the end, a final ruling will be made by a senior lawyer (sometimes advised by someone with a wider social competence such as a court welfare officer) concerning the division of property and the custody and access arrangements for the children. The ruling is legally binding and those who presume to challenge it, except by legal means, risk heavy punishment. Yet judges, and often welfare officers, are repeatedly seen to be working within one particular, rather narrowly bound, view of marriage.

The point of this chapter and the next is to show that both historically and in the present there simply *is* no general consensus about marriage; in fact widely differing views are held about virtually all aspects of the institution. Once this is accepted it may well be easier to see the termination of a marriage not as a disaster or a disgrace but as an occasion for constructive readjustment and further personal growth. Clearly the respondent in our survey who described his divorce as like 'a release from prison' is not alone in this feeling. Such guilt as he may have felt on obtaining his 'release' would have stemmed from his belief in what we have termed the Christian tradition of marriage.

Marriage in the Christian Tradition

Since this is the tradition in which most of us (whether professing Christians or not) were brought up, and since the only formal guidance most people receive concerning the purposes of marriage is that given at the ceremony itself, it seems worthwhile to examine this tradition. 'Christian marriage' may seem to many people to be an idea that is both thoroughly well defined and eternally unchanging. In fact it is neither. Christian teaching about divorce has usually been much more specific than statements about the purpose of marriage. Moreover, within the Christian tradition, doctrine on most of the central issues concerning marriage and divorce has varied radically in different places and different historical epochs. It could almost be said, looked at in the long term, that there *is* no 'Christian marriage'.

The law as laid down, or conveyed, by Moses in Old Testament times dealt more fully with divorce than with marriage. A husband was allowed to divorce his wife, by giving her notice in writing, for reasons such as shameful behaviour or disobedience (see, for example, Deut. 24:1–5 and Esther 1). It seems clear that both the contracting and the ending of a marriage was a private matter (although apparently a wife had to go through a court to divorce her husband) and that the partners were free to remarry. The whole matter seems to have been regarded in a reasonably relaxed matter; in fact the law according to Moses was more precise on issues such as skin disease and on the loss of oxen down wells than on questions of marriage and divorce.

A similarly liberal approach was prevalent under pre-Christian Roman law, (see Kitchin, 1912, upon whom much of the following account is based). Both partners to marriage were treated on an equal footing, little ceremony was involved in marrying and the arrangement was regarded as a civil contract with no great sanctity attached to it. To the Romans, marriage depended above all on mutual affection. Should this cease the marriage too could be terminated without reference to any external authority except where there was dispute about property or children, in which case these issues could be arbitrated by a court. Maintenance payments might well then be ordered, unless the wife had been guilty of misconduct. In fact, though, the wife was not presumed to have any preferential rights over the custody of any children since the degree of guilt, rather than the sex of the parent, seems usually to have been the decisive factor in custody disputes.

In the general context provided by Roman imperial law, Jesus was asked by the Pharisees for his view of marriage and, in particular, whether it was permitted for a husband to divorce his wife. His answer was reported with a variation so significant that it has opened the way for 2000 years of doctrinal division. According to Mark (Mark 10:3–12) Jesus said unambiguously that marriage made the partners 'of one flesh', they were no longer two people but were joined by God and therefore could not be 'put asunder' by any men. If either partner leaves the marriage and marries another he or she commits adultery. Matthew's version of Jesus' words (Matt. 19:3–9) is similar but includes the rather different injunction that any husband who divorces his wife 'except it be for fornication' and then remarries, commits adultery. The obvious implication was that divorce, or 'putting asunder', on the ground of the wife's adultery *is* allowable and remarriage is apparently not then so reprehensible.

In both gospels it is recorded that those listening to Jesus put the obvious point, 'What about the Law of Moses?, Jesus replied that Moses' law provided for men to 'put away' their wives 'because of the hardness of your hearts' but that 'from the beginning it was not so' (Matt. 19:8). Biblical scholars have since debated endlessly not only the specific meaning of 'fornication' but also the broader point of whether the 'Matthean exception' is valid or whether it stems from some misunderstanding, mis-translation or later corruption of the text (see, for example, Montefiore, 1971). If it does, the same invalidity must apply to Matthew's version of the Sermon on the Mount (Matt. 5:31–2) where Jesus' teaching on the question is identically reported.

Some Biblical scholars (for example, Derrett, 1970) have argued that divorce in the one exceptional case apparently allowed by Matthew's version does *not* invalidate the 'one flesh' concept but could be seen as a way of cleansing the family home of an adultress. Whatever interpretation is adopted, there is obviously an uncomfortable ambiguity at the heart of Christian doctrine on marriage and divorce. Does a first marriage render the partners 'of one flesh' forever or does it not?

St Paul's teaching on marriage and divorce, as on other issues of morality, still powerfully influences current opinion, (Grant, 1976). He prefaced his teaching with the wish that everyone could be, like him, a professed celibate (1 Cor. 7) although presumably he was not advocating the logical conclusion of such a doctrine, the extinction of the species. If one could not remain celibate 'it is better to marry than to burn'—and to remain strictly monogamous. And 'let not the wife depart from her husband . . . and let not the husband put away his wife'—thus neatly reinforcing the distinction between the status and expected behaviour pattern of the two partners that had been inherent in Matthew's version of Jesus' teaching. Significantly, St Paul also instructed (I Cor. 7:11) that if the wife *does* depart she should thereafter remain unmarried. It therefore appears that divorce was a known phenomenon, that women sometimes took the initiative in ending the marriage, but that the 'one flesh' concept was an effective prohibition to remarriage in view of the obvious difficulty of being eternally one flesh with more than one other person.

Over the ensuing 2000 years Christian teaching on marriage and divorce has varied significantly as has the effect of this teaching on the codes of law of the many nominally Christian states. Constantine (288–337), as the first Christian emperor of Rome, had to face the awkward problem of incorporating religious teaching on marriage into the state's secular code of law. Legal precision, grounded in a religious doctrine that unfortunately has significant degrees of ambiguity, was required concerning the respective rights of husband and wife. Under the code eventually drawn up by Justinian (483–565), the divorce arrangements owed much to pre-Christian Roman tradition. Divorce could occur by simple consent between the parties with questions of guilt or innocence assuming significance in arbitrating the arrangements concerning children and property.

Following the excommunication of the Eastern Church at Constantinople by Pope Gregory VII in the mid-eleventh century, two sharply contrasting concepts of marriage developed, both nominally Christian. The Eastern or Orthodox Church never made celibacy, even of priests, an essential part of its teaching and divorce was allowable on a variety of grounds. The official line of the Western, or Catholic, Church based on the various decretals, or judgments, by a series of strong Popes, was built into a codified system known as Canon Law. This law was administered by bishops in local ecclesiastical courts and it took a firm line on the sanctity of marriage. Charlemagne, for example, declared marriage to be indissoluble and divorce to be punishable as a crime (although the latter sanction was presumably redundant if the former edict was enforced).

In practice, it seems clear that legally sanctioned separation, followed by life with another partner, could be arranged given sufficient influence with one's bishop and sufficient funds to have the necessary papal dispensation arranged. Alternatively an annulment could be obtained if it could be shown, on any of a number of grounds, that the marriage had been invalid from the beginning. This evidently hypocritical situation whereby a strict doctrinal stance could be circumvented, to the benefit of Church revenues, by the purchase of dispensations was attacked by pens as able as those of Dante, Erasmus, Machiavelli and Martin Luther who finally and publicly burned a copy of the Canon Law in Wittenburg in 1520. Reformers all over northern Europe urged the view, which may sound modern to those unfamiliar with the history of matrimonial law, that marriage was a civil, not a sacramental or spiritual, matter and that it should be dissolvable by mutual consent. In practice the changes they brought about were often to mean simply that a civil judge, rather than a bishop, arbitrated on questions of divorce.

Such developments did not occur in Catholic France until after the 1789 revolution. The revolutionaries' intention was that marriage should become a civil contract and ceremony, with dissolution possible by mutual consent, and with both partners on an equal legal footing. The outcome, the Code drawn up in 1803, managed to combine elements of both Canon Law and revolutionary ideology and it incorporated a need for judicial proceedings in both the making and breaking of marriages. Given that the Code was drawn up largely by lawyers, the cynical may see this latter provision as an attempt to insure against any drop in the lucrative flow of marital litigation.

The law on marriage and divorce in England evolved quite differently. Canon Law on the issue was challenged in the most spectacular way by Henry VIII over the issue of his divorce from Catherine of Aragon. His subsequent excommunication, and his founding of the English church, led to a period of fluctuating attitudes on marriage and divorce under Mary, Edward VI and Elizabeth until the Stuarts reasserted Canon Law with full force. In 1601, the Star Chamber, as the foremost ecclesiastical court in the land, declared a validly constituted marriage to be indissoluble. This did not please the aristocratic and wealthy who, prior to that date, had been able to obtain a divorce by a special Act of Parliament. This method of terminating a marriage, which was often necessary to safeguard family inheritance and succession endangered by a wife's adultery, was restored in 1669 and divorce practice remained virtually unchanged until the mid-nineteenth century. Over these two centuries several hundred men and just four women succeeded in obtaining a divorce (see McGregor, 1957).

The Anglican Church was highly influential in the deliberations of the Royal Commission on questions of marriage which reported in 1853. The bishops were deeply divided; one group led by Bishop Wilberforce maintained that marriage was indissoluble but the main body of Church opinion held to St Matthew's version, allowing divorce and the possible remarriage of the innocent party. The two partners were still expected by some to exhibit differing standards of sexual behaviour since Bishop Wilberforce spoke for many when arguing that adultery was equally sinful in men and women but that in women it was 'a social crime of different magnitude'. Others, notably Lord Lyndhurst (a former Lord Chancellor), Bentham and Mill, argued against the idea of indissolubility, campaigned for the rights of women and generally worked towards the liberalisation of divorce laws. Lord Lyndhurst reached his liberal position following an exhaustive and scholarly review of the arguments advanced by St Augustine *in favour* of indissolubility—another example of the ambiguity possible when even the keenest minds seek to identify the essence of Christian doctrine on the nature of marriage.

The outcome of the theological and legal debates was the 1857 Matrimonial Causes Act which specified the grounds on which a divorce petition could be brought; generally speaking these were solely adultery for a male petitioner but adultery and/or some other marital offence for a female petitioner. The main administrative change lay in the transfer of jurisdiction from Church court to civil courts—a major constitutional event in a state with an established church. To some, such as the Wilberforce faction, all this seemed like a slippery slope at the bottom of which was the spectre of easy divorce for the lower classes in the County Courts.

Following the major social changes of the 1914–18 war, especially those concerning the political and social status of women, Church and State combined to rethink the institution of marriage in the 1920s and 1930s. A strict line on indissolubility was taken by the Anglican hierarchy at a succession of Lambeth Conferences and divorce law reform was opposed not only on the basis of scriptural authority but also, explicitly, on grounds of socio-political stability and public order—a point to be highlighted later in this book. The Archbishops' Joint Committee on Marriage reported in 1935 that marital union was one which could be finally terminated only by death. Similarly the Doctrine Commission set up in 1922 finally concluded in the mid-1930s that marriage is a lifelong union and that grace is divinely accorded to overcome all difficulties.

In the context of Christian Europe since the Reformation, clerical opinion held in England between the wars can reasonably be described as highly reactionary. This encouraged a growing grounds-well of opinion for reform and a growing recognition on the part of more liberal Churchmen that there was an increasing and inevitable divergence between this particular version of Christian doctrine and the feeling among the population at large, many of whom were not practising Christians. The old dilemma of framing a code of law that would satisfy both a doctrinal position and the social realities of an increasingly secular state became acute, as it had in Constantine's Rome and Reformation Europe. In particular, millions were un-happy at the response of the British Church/State establishment to the wish of Edward VIII to marry a twice-divorced American lady. This event, on top of everything else, made reform inevitable. The legislation on divorce that soon emerged, the 1937 Matrimonial Causes Act, (see Herbert, 1937), consolidated by a further Act in 1950, went some way towards meeting the need for reform but even this act did not go far enough to deal with the marital and other upheavals following the 1939–45 war. The stage was therefore set for the lengthy discussions that led to the 1969–71 measures which now legally define the grounds on which marriage can be ended.

Discussions surrounding the present state of the law will be dealt with in Chapter 9. The relevant issue at this point is the part played by Christian opinion, largely in the form of the Anglican Church, in the process of bringing about the current legislation. The group set up by the Archbisop of Canterbury in 1964 was given the task of considering what reforms might be appropriate, taking into account the evident divergence of views between Church and State (as represented by Parliamentary opinion), especially concerning the remarriage of divorced people. In their report, *Putting Asunder* (Mortimer Group, 1966), the group were very clear that their thinking centred on '. . . what the Church ought to say and do about secular laws of marriage and divorce . . .'. They were *not* concerned either to define Christian doctrine or '. . . to impose on the whole nation a law shaped by Christian belief'. This marks a clear retreat from, or perhaps a sensible and realistic reappraisal of, the situation in the pre-Reformation period, the mid-nineteenth century or the inter-war period when the established Church *had* sought to embody its current doctrinal position into the law of the nation.

The question still remains, what precisely does 'Christian marriage' mean? To end this section we should perhaps look briefly at the content of the marriage service itself. In the majestic language of the 1662 *Prayer Book*, marriage signifies '. . . the mystical union that is betwixt Christ and his Church' ordained first '. . . for the pro-creation of children . . .', second '. . . for the remedy against sin, and to avoid fornication . . .' so that those '. . . who have not the gift of continency . . .' may remain undefiled, and third '. . . for the mutual society, help and comfort, that the one ought to have of the other . . .'. It is also significant (in the light of our research findings) that the wife promises to obey the husband and that he, on giving the ring, undertakes to endow her with all his worldly goods. The priest may well preach a sermon at the ceremony but if he does not, the duties of a man and wife are formally spelled out. These make it clear that the two are to be regarded as 'one flesh' so that '. . . he who loveth his wife loveth himself . . .' and that according to St Peter's teaching a man should give honour to his wife '. . . as unto the weaker vessel . . .'. Finally it is made clear that '. . . the husband is the head of the wife, even as Christ is head of the Church . . .'.

Some important changes were made in the *Prayer Book as Proposed in 1928*. References to '. . . men's carnal lusts' and 'fornication' were omitted from the introduction to the service. The vows were made identical for each partner, the word 'obey' was dropped and the husband undertook to 'share' all his worldly goods. It is clear from this proposed revision that the Anglican Church was responding to the post-war changes in society by showing a greater recognition of the rights and status of women while, at the same time, taking a firm line on indissolubility and remarriage. More significant changes were made in the 1980 *Alternative Service Book*, the first major revision of Anglican forms of service for over three centuries. The 'giving away' of a bride became optional and the three main reasons for marriage, while remaining much the same, are set out in the reverse order to the 1662 service. The idea that marriage makes two people 'of one flesh' is still central but as in the 1928 version the vows which the two partners make can exclude the word 'obey' and can be identical to each other. The non-Conformist churches have different services. The *Methodist Service Book* (1975) does not use the phrase 'of one flesh' while that of the United Reformed Church (1980) gives an interesting fourth reason for marriage; it sees the newly married couple as a new creation ready to enter into, and enrich, the life of the community.

To sum up, there is an evident lack of precision about the nature of marriage even within the Christian tradition. Virtually every aspect of the institution, its aims, the property and legal rights of women, the circumstances in which divorce can be granted, the consequent distribution of property and children, the rights to remarriage and so on, all have been very differently pronounced upon in different times and places by different high authorities within nominally Christian systems. When in the next chapter we come to consider the writings of Engels, Reich and some of the feminist authors we shall see that there is perhaps no difficulty in explaining historical variations in doctrine. For the present those seeking a clearer account of why the institution exists, and how one is expected to behave within it may feel they will need to look further afield—perhaps in the writings of sociologists.

Some Sociological Ideas about Marriage and the Family

Sociologists, as the main group of social scientists engaged in the analysis of society, have produced a vast literature on marriage and the family. The main aim in this section will be to summarise the work of some of the more important 'mainstream' authors. Several books provide a good broad review of sociological thinking about marriage including those by Anderson (1971), Shorter (1977) and Morgan (1975). The latter makes the very important point that:

The family is not a formal organization and there is no clearly laid down organizational charter telling people what the family is 'for'.

Thus one present-day sociologist, at least, has rejected the view that there is some divinely ordained rationale for marriage or any 'correct' form of family life. Earlier sociologists, by contrast, had a very clear, almost doctrinally based, view of what marriage ought to be.

The German sociologist Tönnies is regarded as one of the founding fathers of the discipline. In his book *Gemeinshaft und Gesellschaft* first published in 1887 (English translation, Tönnies, 1955) he saw marriage as a special form of what he termed *Gemeinschaft* or close community association based on mutual concern rather than on the hope of deriving some material benefit from others. He saw the mother/child relationship as emotionally the most intense with the husband/father as the natural authority figure always likely to subjugate the 'weaker' adult (the wife) and with a positive authoritative and instructional duty towards the children, especially the eldest son.

Tönnies held that there was a 'natural' division of labour within the household, based on differences in natural strength, such that the woman prepared the food while the man provided the necessities from the outside world and 'warded off enemies'. Nevertheless, one of the 'great main laws' is that '. . . married couples love each other or easily adjust themselves to each other. They speak together and think along similar lines'. Equally, although the various members of the household (husband, wife, children and servants) have their different tasks and 'natural' places of work they are reunited around the table where 'everyone has his place and is given his proper share', thus enjoying jointly the fruits of their separate labour.

In most of these respects Tönnies saw the strongly hierarchical family unit as a desirable miniature version of society at large. He argued that 'all natural authority is concentrated in the paternal authority' which was like that of a prince, landowner or feudal lord and that the study of the household is similar to the study of society just as the study of the organic cell is the study of life itself. Tönnies stressed the close relationship of religion and family life arguing that '. . . religion is family life itself, for the care and assistance given by father or mother is the origin of all divine and godlike guidance . . .'. Predictably he did not approve of the new currents of thought circulating around Europe following the large-scale development of urban industrialised societies. These changes threatened both the life of the small community (because of the new large-scale modes of production in 'factories') and the traditional pattern of marriage (because of the involvement of women in the labour force). In particular he saw a clear connection between the need for ever more complex systems of civil law, much of it owing some debt to Roman legal principles, and the decay of the stable, hierarchical family.

With the woman attaining . . . independence and consequently civic emancipation, marriage and marital community of wealth degenerate into a civil contract.

This in his view, might open the way for dissolution of marriage by mutual consent and further consequent social disintegration.

To many modern minds this view of the marriage relationship in late nineteenth-century Germany no doubt seems totally outdated. Yet it has been echoed in sociological writings until very recent times. The American sociologist Talcott Parsons and his associates wrote much on the family, most of it centred on the middle orders of American society. Their views were summarized in 1955 in the book *Family, Socialization and Interaction Process*. Parsons accepted that war and profound changes in society had exerted pressures on marital relationships but he felt that there was no 'general disorganisation' of family life. He argued that the divorce rate had 'peaked' just after the Second World War and was now on a downward path, that the rising house-building rates were evidence of the strength of the family as a social unit and that there was no serious tendency towards 'symmetry' in the labour market between men and women. In a passage which is a virtual update of Tönnies he argues:

. . . the adult feminine role has not ceased to be anchored primarily in the internal affairs of the family as wife, mother and manager of the household, while the role of the adult male is primarily anchored in the occupational world, in his job and through it by his status-giving and income-earning functions for the family.

On the educational role of the family Parsons writes:

It is because the human personality is not 'born' but must be 'made' through the socialization process that in the first instance families are necessary. They are 'factories' which produce human personalities. . . .

Moreover they are necessary 'for the stablization of the adult personalities of the society'. Parsons argues that a clear distinction between male and female roles is highly desirable and is even a precondition for mature sexual love:

'. . . a mature woman can love, sexually, only a man who takes his full place in the masculine world, above all its occupational aspect . . .'

and he saw evidence at the time that, within the family, the differentiation between the mother's and the father's part in bringing up the children was, if anything, becoming more rather than less significant. He and his associates discussed the potentially bad effects of a breakdown in these traditional arrangements and hinted at a possible link between 'inadequately' distinguished parental roles and the development of schizoid personalities. They also argued that a lack of paternal authority within the family could lead to instability not only in the family but also in the wider society.

Some of the same themes were taken up during the 1950s by writers who were trying to open up the discussion of sex and marriage in ways that were often very radical. By contrast their discussion of sex roles within marriage was very much in line with conventional sociological thinking. Mace, for example, placed heavy emphasis on the desirability of clearly defined sex roles within the home and held strong views on the innate differences between the sexes. He held that 'women are by nature better equipped for self-sacrifice' and that '. . . you owe it to yourself, to your partner, to your children and to society to make a success of your family life' (Mace, 1952).

Macaulay (1957) made it clear that in her view sexual activity could be legitimately engaged in *only* in marriage and that marriage is for the production of children. For women 'there is no career which is of equal importance with that of bearing and rearing children'. Moreover 'the family in which the father takes his share in the upbringing of the children is very fortunate'. Fathers should be primarily sources of authority: '. . . most wives infinitely prefer their husbands to wear the trousers'. Chesser (1957) sounds very modern by comparison. He discussed women's 'love rights', argued that the clergy should be better equipped to deal with marital problems, and raised the issue of the economic value of womens' labour in the home.

Somewhat earlier Murdock had identified four functions of the nuclear family (Murdock, 1949):

  (i) sexual
 (ii) economic
(iii) reproductive
(iv) educational.

Since these functions are obviously crucial for the sheer survival, let alone the well-being, of any society it follows that the nuclear family was an essential institution. He did not argue that it performed all these functions in all societies but rather that there was no other human institution which could fulfil all four together. Murdock made two other claims or assumptions which might be challenged: that factors which strengthen the tie between any two members of a family also strengthen the tie between them and a third member;

and that what is good for society generally (i.e. stable family life) must be good for the individual.

The English sociologist Fletcher, writing in the early 1960s, offered an antidote to the 'alarmists' who were at that time writing of a decline in moral standards, sexual depravity, loss of paternal authority and the general decay of family life (Fletcher, 1962). He saw such fears as both unfounded and 'pessimistic'. He accepted that there was a strong challenge to the notion of marriage as a divinely ordained sacrament and that many now saw it more as a convenient institution for the production and rearing of children. He also accepted that women were gaining a greater degree of educational and economic equality and that with earlier marriage and childbirth many women still had half their life left when the children came of age. But despite all this he argued that marriage was 'natural' because it occurred in virtually all societies. It had, he argued, survived the 1917–36 period in Russia (a period of women's emancipation, easy divorce and abortion and a heavy state role in socialisation, etc.), and that it was surviving well in this country since there was no evidence of any long-term increase in the divorce rate (following the brief post-1945 increase). Fletcher's main message in the early 1960s was that the institution was adjusting well to new external pressures, there were growing levels of co-operation between husband and wife over child-care and that a man's self-respect and significance in the household still depended heavily on his occupational success (or lack of it). If correct, this last point has important implications in any period of high unemployment, which the 1980s seem destined to be.

Coser followed up these themes in 1964, pointing out that one important function of the family was to bestow 'social identity' on its members, almost invariably via the occupation of the father, or 'Head of the Household' (Coser, 1964). Thus the family was the means by which each individual was 'placed' on the social hierarchy until he or she, too, found a place on the ladder independent of the family of origin. Clearly this was, and still is, to some extent true and can be evidenced in the upper echelons of society where mate selection may well depend to some extent on what 'his people' do for a living. It is also formally recognised by the census and other statistical surveys which, without exception, place each household in 'class' categories by using the occupation of the 'head of household'.

More recently Gorer carried out a large survey of attitudes to marriage (Gorer, 1971). This study plotted the differences in attitude between 1950 and 1969 by asking much the same questions (but to a different set of people) in the two years in question. In 1950 there was a very strong feeling that it was desirable to maintain distinct sex roles within the family and the *complementarity* of the two partners was stressed as was the importance of being good at one's particular role. A happy marriage was generally seen as one with enough material comforts and financial security, one where the partners were even-tempered and just got on well.

By 1969, material possessions were taken much for more granted (the standard of living having risen considerably), much more value was placed on *symmetry* as a desirable feature with emphasis on equality, discussion and doing things together. But traditional sex roles seemed clearly to underlie what the two sexes looked for in a marriage partner: men looked for a woman who could be a good parent, housekeeper and cook while women valued qualities such as understanding, affection, thoughtfulness and generosity—evidence of the implicit acceptance of a subsidiary economic role. For both sexes all these qualities rated far above intelligence.

Strangely very little explicit emphasis was placed in either year on sexual compatibility as a good quality in a marriage although marital faithfulness was held as highly desirable, both in 1950 and 1969 (with 92 per cent expressing strong disapproval of extra-marital affairs in the latter year). Since the man's sexual drive was seen to be somewhat stronger than the woman's, affairs by the man were seen as slightly more tolerable than by a woman. A final revealing point from this study (which sampled the opinion of over 2000 people) was that men mentioned children as an important ingredient of a good marriage far more often than did women.

There is, of course, a mass of other important sociological writing on marriage and the family, including work by Ariès (1962), Goode (1963), Harris (1969), Bell (1969) and the various works by Young and Willmott. The overall impression is similar to that gained when reviewing Christian pronouncements on marriage: we are left without any clear consensus on the precise aims and meaning of marriage and family life. Some see the institution as a factory that produces human personalities, some as a means of placing people on the status hierarchy, some as a device for regulating sexual activity and some as a prime means by which the social order and social stability are preserved. No doubt one could conclude lamely that it is something of all these. But it also serves other purposes and can be interpreted in completely different ways as the next chapter will seek to show.

Chapter 2
Marriage—Some Critical Opinions

*The people who defend the institution of marriage
on principle never think of enquiring about its
history and social function*
        W. Reich, The Sexual Revolution

The tradition of critical writing about marriage and the family has its
most obvious source in the work of Engels. It has continued through
Reich and his followers in the 1930s and 1940s, Laing, Esterson and
Cooper in the 1960s and 1970s, and has found its sharpest edge in
the feminist writers of the past two decades inspired perhaps most
clearly by Simone de Beauvoir. This body of writing seems to spring
from a quite different intellectual world to that inhabited by
churchmen or mainstream sociologists. While on the whole far less
concerned with precise documentation (often in this case a diver-
sionery activity), these writers are at their best, more piercing in
their analyses, more politically aware in their approach and more
ready to see the illuminating links between the nature of the institution of marriage at any given time and the particular economic and
political system in which it exists (see also Poster, 1978, for a useful
discussion of this issue).

Engels

Engels provides a convenient starting point in his long essay *The
Origin of the Family, Private Property and the State*, originally
published in 1884. The essay was prompted partly by the then
recently published book *Ancient Society* by L. H. Morgan (1877).
This work was typically Victorian in its massive historical sweep
through human history, using a three-stage analysis, proceeding
from savagery, through barbarism to civilisation. Equally important
contributory ideas stemmed from the earlier communitarian and
feminist writings of Robert Owen and his followers, some of whom

sought to remodel marriage relationships in their new communities (Taylor, forthcoming 1983). Engels was stimulated to enlarge on some of these startling new ideas about monogamous marriage. He developed especially the notion that marriage was *not* some divinely ordained and eternally appropriate institution, rather it was an inevitable outgrowth of another, historically specific, institution— inheritable private property. The point is important enough to justify some extensive quotations.

Following a discussion of earlier systems of marriage such as polygamy (where a man had several wives), polyandry (the common possession of a woman by a number of men), group marriage and 'pair marriage' (a transient and easily dissolved form of monogamy), Engels arrives at the growth of the lifelong monogamous, or as he terms it monogamian, marriage:

It is based on the supremacy of the man; its express aim is the begetting of children of undisputed paternity, this paternity being required in order that these children may in due time inherit their father's wealth as his natural heirs. The monogamian family differs from pairing marriage in the far greater rigidity of the marriage tie, which can now no longer be dissolved at the pleasure of either party. Now, as a rule, only the man can dissolve it and cast off his wife. The right of conjugal infidelity remains his even now, sanctioned, at least, by custom (the Code Napoleon expressly concedes this right to the husband as long as he does not bring his concubine into the conjugal home), and is exercised more and more with the growing development of society. Should the wife recall the ancient sexual practice and desire to revive it, she is punished more severely than ever before. We are confronted with this new form of the family in all its severity among the Greeks.

Engels illustrates this point with reference to classical Greek writings. He goes on:

This was the origin of monogamy, as far as we can trace it among the most civilised and highly-developed people of antiquity. It was not in any way the fruit of individual sex love, with which it had absolutely nothing in common, for the marriages remained marriages of convenience, as before. It was the first form of the family based not on natural but on economic conditions, namely, on the victory of private property over original, naturally developed, common ownership. The rule of the man in the family, the procreation of children who could only be his, destined to be the heirs of his wealth—these alone were frankly avowed by the Greeks as the exclusive aims of monogamy. For the rest, it was a burden, a duty to the gods, to the state and to their ancestors, which just had to be fulfilled. In Athens the law made not only marriage compulsory, but also the fulfilment by the man of a minimum of the so-called conjugal duties. Thus, monogamy does not by any means make its appearance in history as the reconciliation of man and woman, still less as the highest form of such a reconciliation. On the contrary, it appears as the subjection of one sex by the other, as the proclamation of a conflict between the sexes entirely unknown hitherto in prehistoric times.

Given human nature as he understood it, Engels maintained that apart from oppression within the marriage at least two other social institutions were always bound to co-exist with monogamous property-based marriage; these were adultery and prostitution (on both of which Engels might be said to have been a sound first-hand reporter).

To illustrate the point from contemporary society Engels contrasted marriage among the bourgeois classes with sexual relations among the poor (so vividly written up forty years earlier in his classic account of life in Manchester in *The Condition of the Working Class in England*). At the bourgeois level, he argued, arranged marriage was common in the Catholic countries, and divorce had been abolished since the church had become resigned to the view that '. . . for adultery, as for death, there is no cure whatsoever'. The Protestant countries allowed sons to seek wives for themselves which still

'. . . leads merely, if we take the average of the best cases, to a wedded life of leaden boredom, which is described as domestic bliss'.

For the poor it was different, sexually based love could be more natural and free:

Sex love in the relation of husband and wife is and can become the rule only among the oppressed classes, that is, at the present day, among the proletariat, no matter whether this relationship is officially sanctioned or not. But here all the foundations of classical monogamy are removed. Here, there is a complete absence of all property, for the safeguarding and inheritance of which monogamy and male domination were established. Therefore, there is no stimulus whatever here to assert male domination.

Engels produced no hard social scientific evidence to substantiate these conclusions; but they were based on close participant observation in a number of European cities over nearly five decades. Moreover he felt that legislators all over Europe were recognising that, to be effective, marriage must serve the deepest interests of both parties and that 'both parties must be on an equal footing in respect to rights and obligations'. Yet there was, in his view, a long way to go before women got anywhere near re-emancipation. The move from communistic group households to privatised mono-gamous family living had made the wife 'the first domestic servant'. Modern large-scale industry had enabled her to regain her former significance by selling her independent labour power in some form of employment. But even then she was expected to carry out the bulk of the domestic labour as well—a point no doubt familiar to countless women today.

Looking to the future, Engels considered that in the social and economic revolution predicted by Marxist theory, the economic foundations of monogamy (private inheritable wealth) would dis-appear; *so, therefore, would the ideal of lifelong monogamous marriage.* Most wealth and other assets would be socially owned and communally used so there would be no anxiety about inheritance. The idea of indissoluble marriage, the product of a particular form of production and wealth distribution 'exaggerated by religion' would wither away—it had, in any event, been 'breached a thousandfold'. In a final telling passage, which it is still difficult to dispute in the light of survey findings, Engels reached much the same conclusion as the Romans;

If only marriages that are based on love are moral, then, also only those are moral in which love continues. The duration of the urge of individual sex love differs very much according to the individual, particularly among men; and a definite cessation of affection, or its displacement by a new passionate love, makes separation a blessing for both parties as well as for society. People will only be spared the experience of wading through the useless mire of divorce proceedings.

Engels' key contribution (following Morgan) to the analysis of marriage and the family was perhaps his insistence that these were *changing* institutions. He argued that historically the regulation of sexual relations and the arrangements for the care of the young (and thus the reproduction of the society from one generation to the next) have changed as a response to changes in economic conditions and especially as a response to developments in the *form* of com-modity production, and the extent to which the *means* of production and the products themselves are privately owned. This is a direct contradiction to the teaching of Jesus with its apparently ahistorical insistence on lifelong monogamous marriage as an eternal ideal state regardless of, or with no attention paid to, other social and economic considerations. When confronted with the 'divorce explosion' of the 1970s and early 1980s it seems deeply significant that few, if any, of the partners entering marriage had been encouraged, or even effectively allowed, to reflect on these diametrically opposed concepts of marriage as they passed through eleven years or more of formal education.

As was the case in most fields of social and economic analysis, the work of Marx and Engels (in this case primarily the latter) had profound effects on ideas about marriage and the family. In particular, post-revolutionary Russia attempted a full-scale 'sexual revolution'. As might be expected, the law under the Czars had taken a very traditional view of marriage (see Reich, 1951), with the husband legally bound to love his wife (Article 106), the wife bound to obey her husband (Article 107), parents to have power over their children up to any age (Article 164), and even power to have them imprisoned for disobedience (Article 165). Soon after the revolution, in December 1917, Lenin issued decrees concerning sex equality and there followed a string of further laws which made marriage a private matter and divorce obtainable on almost any grounds. Alimony was virtually abolished at a stroke, although the necessary economic concomitant of such a measure, the ability of women to support themselves in the labour market, could not be generated overnight. Birth control measures were vigorously enacted and abortion was legalised, but only as a necessary step to reduce illegal abortions and as a stop-gap until birth control policies could effectively regulate population growth. In addition many experiments were started to develop collective living such as youth communes in some of which all goods, even clothes, were owned in common.

Reich

Wilhelm Reich, the Austrian psychiatrist and follower of Freud, was a sympathetic observer of this attempt to implement a new approach to marriage and family life in Russia. He saw, as many others did, that deep-seated traditions of monogamy and child care within the nuclear family cannot be overturned in a year or so even by a series of edicts from a Leninist ruling élite. He noted the confusion and resentment caused by the rapidity of this attempt to impose a sexual revolution and he drew a number of conclusions when many of these policies were completely reversed in the mid-

1930s. His book *The Sexual Revolution* was first published in 1930 and again, in an enlarged form, in 1936. Later editions appeared in 1944 and 1949, by which time he had moved to the United States.

His intellectual point of departure was a criticism of his mentor Freud. Reich accepted the validity of Freud's distinction between the 'pleasure principle' (an expression of our primary and unrestrained wants and needs) and the 'reality principle' (our recognition that we cannot indulge all these impulses, except in fantasy, because we live in a society where others have rights). The tension is one between basic instincts and 'civilised' codes of behaviour. Reich believed, however, that Freud had written as if the degree to which this tension was felt was *historically unvarying* whereas in Reich's view the degree of tension, and thus the degree of guilt felt on indulging the 'pleasure principle', *did* vary in different historical periods—in particular it depended upon the degree of repression in the state's laws concerning marriage, divorce, extra-marital sexual relations, child sexuality and the role of women.

In Reich's view the society around him, dominated by bourgeois ethics and repressive legislation, was sexually sick. The approach to sexual morality, marriage and child-rearing inherent in 'ecclesiastical, fascist and other reactionary ideologies' was described (in a passage that seems pure D. H. Lawrence) as a defence mechanism against 'the unconscious inferno which everyone carries within himself'. Reich's central point was that moral regulation of instinctual life, if the morality is not founded on sound principles, 'creates exactly what it pretends to master: antisocial impulses'. The discussion therefore hinges on what 'sound principles' of morality might be.

To Reich it seemed necessary to create a society where *natural* sexual needs could be met without fear of repression at any level. Such a society

Would, for example, not only not prohibit a love relationship between adolescents; it would give its full protection and help. It would, for example, not only not prohibit infantile masturbation; it would deal severely with any adult who would prevent the child from developing its natural sexuality.

Reich termed such a society 'sex-economic'. It would recognise the life-affirmative nature of sexual instincts and the need to gratify them within broadly social limits without the negative effects of repressive, authoritarian or hypocritical legislation based on incomplete visions of human sexuality. Such legislation can only produce more guilt, more 'distortion' of human nature and more anti-social behaviour.

By contrast, a society based on a 'sex-economic' morality would be largely self-regulatory in sexual matters. It would facilitate the ideal of repeated sexual satisfaction with the same partner, thus making lifelong relationships more, rather than less, likely and it would obviate both sexual frustration within marriage and an irrepressible search for satisfaction outside it:

The essence of sex-economic regulation lies in the avoidance of any absolute norms or precepts and in the recognition of the will to life and pleasure in living as the regulators of social life. The fact that today, due to the disordered human structure, this recognition is reduced to a minimum does not speak against the principle of self-regulation; on the contrary, it speaks against the moral regulation which has created this pathological structure.

Even the so-called 'reformers' of the time were, to Reich, impossibly reactionary. He quoted one such, Gruber, who wrote:

We have to cultivate woman's chastity as the highest national possession, for it is the only safe guarantee that we really are going to be the fathers of our children, that we work and labor for our own flesh and blood. Without this guarantee there is no possibility of a secure family life, this indispensable basis for the welfare of the nation. This, and not masculine selfishness, is the reason why the law and morals make stricter demands on the woman than on the man with regard to premarital chastity and to marital fidelity. Freedom on her part involves much more serious consequences than freedom on the part of the man.

Reich considered, exactly as Engels had, that this philosophy completely confused the issue of natural love with that of property and inheritance. It created tensions which could be relieved only by adultery, prostitution, double standards, personal guilt and self-repression.

As we have seen, Reich regarded stable fulfilling marriage as a desirable ideal but he certainly did not approve of the majority of marriages he saw around him. He termed them 'authoritarian compulsive marriages', products of and supporters of the authoritarian society and state. In anticipation of a phrase of Talcott Parsons he saw them as 'factories for authoritarian ideologies'. Nor were they happy. Making reference to a nineteenth-century study which identified very few marriages that were both happy and faithful, and to a later study by Bloch which found only fifteen out of one hundred 'undoubtedly happy' (and in thirteen of these there had been some unfaithfulness), Reich carried out his own survey in 1925. Of ninety-three marriages with which he was 'well acquainted' he found only three to be happy. One must, of course, approach such findings by a practising psychiatrist with some caution since his sample is unlikely to be fully representative but the indications are still striking. Reich's conclusion was that:

. . . the prevailing sexual misery is due to the conflict between natural sexual needs on the one hand and the ideology of extramarital abstinence and lifelong monogamous marriage on the other hand.

For Reich, the way forward towards a stable and sexually fulfilled society, and to enduring marriage, lay in moving towards the economic independence of women and in developing natural and tender mutual love based on pleasurable sexual experiences. This depended on avoiding guilt feelings in early sexual development and the capacity to develop awareness of the sexual needs of others, and of one particular other person. It also involved a recognition that some 'dulling' will occur from time to time in the relationship with the partner since 'sexual interest cannot be commanded'. The best chance of preserving the relationship lay in recognising the desire for others as natural and not letting the understandable feelings of jealousy turn into possessive demands should it be indulged for a period.

Reich made two final significant points. It is normally assumed that Christian doctrine invariably specifies monogamous marriage as not only in accord with divine guidance but also as some kind of natural human state. Yet Reich drew attention to an edict issued by Nurnberg District Council on 14 February 1650 (St Valentine's Day) following the loss of population suffered in the Thirty Years' War:

Whereas the needs of the Holy Roman Empire make it necessary to replace again the manhood which during this Thirty Years' War has been decimated by the sword, sickness and hunger . . . every male, for the next ten years, shall, therefore be allowed to marry two women.

Clearly in some circumstances practical considerations have come before crucial elements of teaching since it is difficult to reconcile this edict with the 'one flesh' doctrine. The second point is one that grows naturally out of Engels' arguments and which has in turn been powerfully developed in recent feminist writings about the role of women in mature capitalist systems:

Owing to the economic dependence of the women on the man and her lesser gratification in the processes of production, marriage is a protective institution for her, but at the same time she is exploited in it. For she is not only the sexual object of the man and the provider of children for the state, but her unpaid work in the household indirectly increases the profit of the employer. For the man can work at the usual low wages only on the condition that in the home so and so much work is done without pay. If the employer were responsible for the running of his workers' homes, he either would have to pay a housekeeper for them or would have to pay them wages which would allow the workers to hire one. This work, however, is done by the housewife, without remuneration.

Laing

The next critical tradition to be considered is also rooted in psychoanalysis but is somewhat different both in its approach to the internal 'politics' of the family and to the relationship of the family to the outside world. R. D. Laing trained in medicine and then in psychiatry but during the 1960s and 1970s he developed a critique of family dynamics which is sharply different from that of more conventional psychiatry. His concentration on the family developed out of a broader interest in the condition generally known as schizophrenia, a term which he uses with some disquiet in view of its 'catch-all' nature (Laing, 1967).

In using the term schizophrenia, I am not referring to any condition that I suppose to be mental rather than physical, or to an illness, like pneumonia, but to a label that some people pin on other people under certain social circumstances.

Laing is somewhat more unhappy with the world at large than he is with 'schizophrenics'. We have, he argues, had to make a number of damaging adjustments to ourselves in order to cope with the violence and irrationality of world events:

In the last fifty years, we human beings have slaughtered by our own hands coming on for one hundred million of our species. We all live under constant threat of our total annihilation. We seem to seek death and destruction as much as life and happiness. We are as driven to kill and be killed as we are to let live and live. Only by the most outrageous violation of ourselves have we achieved our capacity to live in relative adjustment to a civilization apparently driven to its own destruction.

Perhaps, argues Laing, schizophrenia is in some cases '. . . a successful attempt *not* to adopt to pseudo realities . . .'. Perhaps:

The perfectly adjusted bomber pilot may be a greater threat to species survival than the hospitalized schizophrenic deluded that the Bomb is inside him.

Perhaps, anyway,

There is no such 'condition' as 'schizophrenia', but the label is a social fact and the social fact a *political event* [Laing's own emphasis],

a point which is unfortunately developed only in terms of welfare provision rather than in relation to the broader political system.

Laing and his associates carried out many case studies of the family situation of patients referred to him as schizophrenic (see Laing and Esterson, 1964). These cases focussed his attention firmly on the nuclear family which, for a variety of reasons, he found a baffling field of study (Laing, 1971):

The more one studies family dynamics, the more *un*clear one becomes as to the ways *family* dynamics compare and contrast with the dynamics of other groups not called families, let alone the ways families themselves differ.

The family is not just a 'we' within and a 'them' outside. It is a complex system of sub-groups consisting of individuals and pairs, each individual having his or her own unique self-perception and a unique perception of each of the other members, sub-groups and pair-relationships. In his emphasis on the family as *experienced* by its members, Laing acknowledges his debt to Sartre. The functions of the family and the relationships within it cannot be set out in any objective way; they are subjectively experienced and then internalised.

'Internalization' means to map 'outer' onto 'inner'. It entails the transference of a group of relations constituting a set (with a number of operations within the set between elements of the set, products remaining in the set) from one modality of experience to others: namely from perception to imagination, memory and dreams.

The 'group mode' experienced within the family, the particular way of relating, now 'mapped' within the individual, is transferred over to the outside world.

Transference entails carrying over one metamorphosis, based on being 'in' and having inside oneself one group mode of sociality, into another.

The family acts as a defence against '. . . collapse, disintegration, emptiness, despair, guilt and other terrors'. But it also stifles individual growth by a process Laing calls 'attribution' whereby children (principally) are led, almost hypnotised, into beliefs about themselves projected by parents. This control over the development of children is based less on what they are explicitly told to *do*, more on what they are implicitly led to believe they *are*. Thus

His parents tell him he *is* naughty, because he does not do what they tell him. What they tell him *is*, is *induction*, far more potent than what they tell him to do. Thus through the attribution: 'You are naughty', they are effectively telling him *not to do* what they are ostensibly telling him to do.

For example:

'He's so naughty. He never does what I tell him. Do you?

'I keep telling him to be more careful, but he's so careless, aren't you?

he considers this process of attribution to be so powerful that:

I consider many adults (including myself) are or have been, more or less, in a hypnotic trance, induced in early infancy: we remain in this state until— when we dead awaken, as Ibsen makes one of his characters say—we shall find that we have never lived.

As a final example of the stifling and repressive power of love as applied in an everyday family situation, and not necessarily in any 'deviant' or 'pathological' case, Laing reproduces the following conversation between a mother and her daughter and adds his piercing interpretation of it:

M (to fourteen-year-old daughter): You are evil.
D: No, I'm not.
M: Yes, you are.
D: Uncle Jack doesn't think so.
M: He doesn't love you as I do. Only a mother really knows the truth about her daughter, and only one who loves you as I do will ever tell you the truth about yourself no matter what it is. If you don't believe me, just look at yourself in the mirror carefully and you will see that I'm telling the truth.

The daughter did, and saw that her mother was right after all, and realized how wrong she had been not to be grateful for having a mother who so loved her that she would tell her the truth about herself. Whatever it might be.
What, I think, we find most immediately disturbing about this can be expressed in general terms as follows: the other person induces self to map into self's own image of self a value which we feel, should not be mapped onto self; the self-system is a range that should not, we may feel, be mapped in that way, in any circumstances or only under extreme circumstances.

Morgan (1975) has aptly summed up Laing's contribution to the analysis of the family:

Laing presents us with the dark, unspoken side of family living, a side too readily played down in much of the text-book discussion of the 'functions' of the family. . . . The family is a destructive exploitative institution as much as it is the reverse.

Cooper

Laing has his followers. Cooper is explicitly concerned with the bourgeois nuclear family unit, and especially with the way it functions, in his view, as a conditioning unit in capitalist and other exploitative societies (Cooper, 1971). In one of many dismissive judgments Cooper sees the contemporary bourgeois family as 'the ultimately perfected form of non-meeting'. Its political role is clearly asserted at the beginning of the book in a passage which closely mirrors Gramsci's analysis of the factors that perpetuate ruling ideologies (see Boggs, 1976):

The power of the family resides in its social mediating function. It reinforces the effective power of the ruling class in any exploitative society by providing a highly controllable paradigmatic form for every social institution. So we find the family form replicated through the social structures of the factory, the union branch, the school (primary and secondary), the university, the business corporation, the church, political parties and governmental apparatus, the armed forces, general and mental hospitals, and so on.

Cooper is concerned especially with the way nuclear family living prevents us from existing in a world of our own. We have to live 'agglutinatively'—with bits of other people glued on. The family is destructive of personal development because it reinforces its member's sense of personal incompleteness, it lays down the roles members should play rather than encouraging the free development of identity, it instils in children far more social controls than are necessary to navigate life and it indoctrinates them with an elaborate system of taboos, especially in terms of sensual communication, thus setting up the conditions for massive guilt feelings in later life. For Cooper, the soundest basis on which to establish love is the development of one's separateness. This is precisely what nuclear family living tends to inhibit. It also inhibits the development of self-love which Cooper considers to be an essential part of a genuinely loving relationship with another:

A loving relationship is a relationship in which each person makes it possible for the other to love themselves enough to precondition a development of the relationship. It's all a matter of how one doesn't stop the other person being *nice* and *kind* to herself or himself.

Predictably Cooper regards contractual marriage as the 'submission of personal need to an externally imposed time-scheme'. Our time withers away without our noticing until we feel suddenly that we want it back, which involves 'a devastating shattering of our laboriously erected security structures' in a 'break-up' (and how sharply this analysis is echoed in our research findings). The alternative, of course, is some more communal form of living: a reduced insistence on the stifling exclusivity of conventional marital arrangements. 'The family, as we have seen, is endlessly replicated in its anti-instinctuality throughout all the institutions of this society'.

Cooper's book is deeply-felt and violently compassionate. It provides insight but offers no clearly defined way out of the impasse. It makes passing references to the broader society outside the marriage but gives little practical guidance about the means by which individuals and society alike can be liberated from the destructive effects (as he saw them) of permanent, exclusive monogamy. The only way out is divorce which often carries with it 'false resentment instead of real gratitude—*But then the only evil of divorce is the prior evil of marriage*' (Cooper's emphasis). Perhaps it is asking too much to call for solutions; very few people can be both sensitively insightful about personal relationships and skilled in social analysis and policy advocacy.

Some Feminist Writers

Perhaps if any group has managed to combine analysis at these two levels it is the formidable set of feminist authors whose work is most obviously rooted in Engels. They have a lot to write about: the patriarchal authoritarian nature of family structures (which carries Biblical endorsement); the long-standing subordination of women in social, cultural and economic spheres; the double standards exemplified in the expectation that, on marriage, the woman should be virginal and the man experienced; and the massive lack of sexual self-awareness no doubt experienced by millions of women and summed up in the poignant observation: 'He's very good, he doesn't bother me much' (quoted in Morgan, 1975).

It is difficult, perhaps insulting, to seek to summarise this literature in a few paragraphs but certain basic themes emerge strongly. Simone de Beauvoir writes of the need for marriage to be a coming together of two individuals, each whole and independent, who will continue to be integrated in society at large, rather than two people who will sink their identity in some 'closed cell' (de Beauvoir, 1953). In her view most contemporary marriages are nothing like her ideal. Unless they are, the obvious remedy for the woman who seeks to retain and develop her identity is divorce. The ease and self-respect with which this can be achieved depends upon the economic system and the possibilities for women to support themselves within it, for alimony payments, however set, are widely resented by both sexes alike (if for different reasons).

The issue of discrimination against women in the labour market is both simple and complex. There is no doubt whatsoever that women almost always run a greater risk of economic exploitation than men, certainly in all capitalist systems and probably in many socialist ones. Equal pay legislation has been widely enacted and has produced measurable change, but it is not totally effective (as the continuing difference between average male and female earnings indicates). Much of the debate in the feminist literature (see Kuhn and Wolpe, 1978) has been about the extent to which this inequality is an inevitable by-product of the particular form of economic organisation through which we are now passing (mature industrialised capitalism).

The 'trade cycles' inherent in capitalist production (although clearly not exclusive to this economic system) require an 'industrial reserve army' of labour which can be enlisted when economic activity is near the top of the cycle and laid off in times of business recession (see Marx, 1976, Chapter 25). Women are prime sufferers in this process, which has obvious implications for their long-term economic security as individuals. But at the time of writing (1982), under an administration making a clinically cool use of unemployment to 'restructure' the economy, it would be wrong to emphasise the special sufferings of women in the labour market. Up to two million men are also unemployed, and some of the damage that unemployment inflicts on marital relationships can be glimpsed from the survey findings.

Much debate has also been centred on the extent to which, at the personal level, the sexual 'power balance' (which involves, by implication, important areas of male domination) is something inherent or 'natural' as opposed to something rooted in particular historical circumstances. To Firestone it is certainly the latter; and historical circumstances can be changed. The problem of women's emancipation is therefore largely a political one; the subordinate role is not part of any natural order:

Thus the 'natural' is not necessarily a 'human' value. Humanity has begun to transcend Nature: we can no longer justify the maintenance of a discriminatory sex class system on grounds of its origins in nature. Indeed, for pragmatic reasons alone it is beginning to look as if we *must* get rid of it (Firestone, 1979).

But what is to be done about the 'origins in nature'? Women bear the children and a whole set of child-care consequences tend to flow from this. Or need they? For Firestone part of the political programme is for women to gain greater control over their reproductive role and thus to combat not only their own repression but also the ecological dangers of large-scale population growth. This concern leads to an interest, shared by most feminist writers, in experiments in alternative forms of social organisation, child-care and education (she discusses in particular the Russian 'sexual revolution', the Israeli Kibbutz and A. S. Neill's Summerhill, a famous experiment in self-regulating education).

Another line of argument advanced by the feminists develops the point made by Engels and others that the Industrial Revolution changed the way in which many commodities (for example, textiles and metal goods) were produced and in doing so it changed the *social relations* of production. Home-based activity, in which the women and children played an important part, was substituted by factory-based production. In the new situation, women could either sell their labour (at exploitative rates) to the factory owners or they could take on a purely 'servicing' role, privatised within the home, as producers of children to form the next generation of wage labourers and as domestic provides of food and other essential services for the men of the household. It follows, given the significance of this domestic labour to the economic prosperity of the system, that the question of payment for these services will arise. There should, it has been argued, be a wage payment direct to the woman rather than, say, an informal sharing of the husband's income (as practised in the majority of marriages) or a welfare payment made by the state (such as a child benefit). The arguments for this payment are currently being clarified in the course of a lively debate between various advocates of the same principle (see Kuhn and Wolpe, 1978).

The growth and 'visibility' of feminist arguments may help some men to make sense of what is otherwise a bewildering and hurtful experience, the sudden and unexpected militancy, even viciousness, of a wife seeking a divorce. Many men simply cannot understand what is happening when their marriage, long established and materially secure, begins to be threatened by evident signs of discontent in the wife. The bewilderment is compounded on receipt of strongly worded legal documents drawn up by lawyers who, all too often, encourage the inclusion of any arguments or episodes, suitably embroidered, which they feel will benefit their clients' interests. In many cases the explanation (discounting for a moment the sometimes unhelpful effects of the lawyers) is that the woman has gradually been experiencing a growing awareness of her subservient role, a role into which she was socialised from infancy and which has been reinforced in many of her dealings with teachers, employers, and male friends. Some event or realisation causes her to reflect on the growing discrepancy between her own educational, social, sexual or economic aspirations and the marital straitjacket in which she may (or of course may not) feel she is entangled. She need not have read Millett, Greer, de Beauvoir or Mitchell, probably only a minority of people have, but these writers are just the articulate 'sharp end' of what is probably a massive body of feeling.

The difference between these new versions of the relationship between the sexes and the version into which most of us were socialised is considerable and it can produce severe internal tension. At the level of the individual marriage, this tension may be resolved by open discussion, and facilitating adjustments by the husband (for example, by changing the balance of household chores to enable the wife to take on a job or work on a correspondence course). But this adjustment may not be enough, it may not be offered at all, or the reaction may be negative and defensive. In such cases it is not surprising that there follows a hostile explosion of feelings; the woman's hazily-grasped but deeply-felt resentment of years of conformity to prevailing norms, triggered by some release mechanism, catapults itself at the nearest target—the husband. He, perhaps as much a victim of the conventional role expectations as his wife, makes little sense of it, responds in kind, and the battle is on.

The difference between the competing conceptions of marriage outlined in this and the previous chapter is so great that perhaps in the end it is surprising that so *few* divorces have occurred in the last decade rather than so many. Everywhere there are confusions in a key area of life where one hopes for a clear 'model' to work to. There are many competing models and they raise many questions. How much guilt should be felt by practising Christians who marry in Church and vow lifelong fidelity only to find as time goes on that they need to part because they are destroying each other? To what extent should non-Christians who take Christian marriage vows be governed by them? Was Reich more perceptive than Christian doctrine about the essential nature of human sexuality when he argued that on occasion extra-marital sexual experiences might have a positive effect on a marriage? Should a woman who leaves the daily care of her children to someone else while she pursues her career feel guilty (as conventional morality would argue) if she does—or guilty if she doesn't, because she is failing to develop herself fully as a person? Does the secret of a happy marriage, as Cooper and Simone de Beauvoir have argued, lie in the coming together of two people who preserve their own self-love and their links with society at large? Or do marriage and sexual relations entail the two becoming 'one flesh' for life and perhaps beyond (and surely Hardy's Tess was not the only woman whose life was destroyed by this belief)? Does an upbringing in a home with 'inadequately' distinguished parental sex roles increase the risk that one will become schizoid (as Parsons argues)? Or is the root cause of many schizophrenic conditions to be found in precisely the sort of family life that Parsons appeared to approve (as Laing would argue)? And finally should women who actually feel perfectly happy and fulfilled in a conventional wife/mother role feel some inadequacy because they fail to be angry at the way they are being exploited (to accept for a moment the arguments from Engels to the latest feminist writing)?

There seems to be no straight answer to any of these questions and no blanket prescriptions for marital success. Clearly, at the moment, these issues are being worked through by trial and error in literally millions of marriages. In many cases the 'errors' end up, with enormous pain and anger, in the divorce courts. Perhaps the only thing one can say with fair certainty is that trial and error is not a good procedure here. It would seem helpful for those who intend to marry to have some knowledge of the range of ideas concerning the institution *before* they contract a marriage so that they might at least understand each other's position on the questions raised. There appears, at present, to be no systematic way of encouraging this prior discussion. Sexually mature teenagers leave school with more knowledge of algebra and the kings and queens of England than of alternative perspectives on marriage and the family.

Private Misery or Public Issue?

As we have seen, there is little common ground between the various views on marriage and the family. But in one significant respect nearly all of them are in agreement: they recognise the close relationship between what is happening within the family and what is happening in society at large. This recognition is shared by both thinkers and men of action. Napoleon was a strong upholder of the family because he understood that the state can be more easily ruled when family life is stable and the husband the absolute head of the household unit. The patriarchal family and the hierarchical state are mutually supportive. Present-day politicians, although they might not state it so transparently, share this belief and both main parties in Britain claim to be 'the party of the family'. Other régimes have taken a different view. The ruling élite in post-Revolutionary Russia, the Nazi Party in Germany and the rulers of the new post-war state of Israel, all sought to undermine the family, or at least to encourage alternative, more communal, ways of living. But they were each seeking to reinforce new revolutionary or nationalistic ideologies and they saw the family as a force for reaction which had to be undermined. Administrations that seek to *preserve* the status quo seek also to preserve the patriarchal nuclear family.

This point is made quite clear by the statements of those involved in producing new family legislation in Britain. The Denning Committee (1947) argued that 'the marriage tie is of the highest importance in the interests of society' and it called for a strong state policy on the family. The Finer Committee on one-parent families called marriage '. . . an institution central to society . . .' and held that:

The family is the basic institution which . . . ensures, in the course of socialising the young, the transmission of ethical and cultural values across the generations (Finer Committee, 1974).

Following a discussion of the role of the law in enforcing various marital rights and obligations it argues: 'In all this the first and dominant purpose of the law is to uphold the family'.

There are several reasons why this general emphasis on family stability should be repeatedly stressed in governmental and other official statements. The *Finer Report* draws attention to the financial circumstances of one-parent families and the expensive welfare provision that has to be made for them from public funds. For example, it is currently estimated that one-parent families reliant on Supplementary Benefit (a minority of one-parent families) cost £215 million per year via this source alone (*Social Trends*, 1982). In addition the *Finer Report* reviews the research work that clearly demonstrates the disproportionate educational and other difficulties experienced by children in one-parent families. Following on the same theme, the Working Party on Marriage Guidance in their consultative document *Marriage Matters* (1979) spell out the rationale for stronger state initiatives to protect marriage and the family. They point out:

The cost of marital disharmony is felt not only in terms of human suffering but in the economy. The cost of dealing with marital disharmony is enormous.

This must be true, although we have been unable to locate any studies that have even begun to assess this economic cost.

The issue is not simply one of *public* finance. The nuclear family of father, mother and 2.3 children is the prime unit of consumption for a vast range of commodities. It is therefore the 'target' purchasing unit for products ranging from breakfast cereals in 'family packs' through consumer durables and motor cars to the most expensive and necessary product of all—housing. What effects would a sudden mass move towards communal living, balanced at the other extreme by a large increase in the number of one or two-person households, have on the sale of freezers, family cars and many other commodities designed over the years to be suitable for the needs of four to five-person consumption units? In the field of housing there is a two-stage reinforcement for the marital status quo. Not only is the vast proportion of housing units designed for family occupation but the basis on which they are occupied has changed from about one-tenth owner-occupied in 1914 to about 55 per cent. Thus the majority of married couples are locked into joint long-term financial commitments via mortgage loans. These arrangements have immensely complicated the process of breaking up a family unit and are an additional cause for tension, bitterness and litigation when a marriage dissolution occurs. Not for nothing has the growth of owner-occupancy over the last sixty years been powerfully fostered by successive governments with financial concessions to house purchase that have cost the state far more than the subsidies to local authority tenants; home ownership has been declared 'a bulwark against bolshevism' by more than one leading politician (Bellman, 1928). The 'regular' stable family unit of Mum, Dad and the kids with their mortgage commitments as a 'stake in the system', and with aspirations towards a steadily growing set of consumer durables, is an essential support both to the politics of reaction and to the production system which has carefully geared itself to their pattern of demand.

But it may well be that the rapidly rising divorce rate is beginning to have some de-stabilising effects. Since the change in the divorce law in January 1971, just over one million divorces have occurred and the curve is still rising. This means that in the last ten years two million adults and over a million children have had first-hand experience of the anger and sadness of a marital break-up. The pervasive effects of this historically unprecedented situation have not been seriously researched. One obvious demographic effect is a move towards smaller average household size since typically, for a period, a three-person and a one-person household will replace one four-person household. The disposable income of each of the two consequent spending units will probably be lower than that of the original household (until, possibly, a remarriage occurs). The children may well grow up in a one-parent home with their conception of the way adults relate to each other heavily influenced by the mutual anger which almost inevitably will be exhibited by the two adults they love most. For many of them, father will have become a partly discredited, remote figure, perhaps no longer to be regarded with respect, someone who has 'lost out' in some imperfectly grasped power struggle, in short the opposite of the ideal envisaged by Tönnies and Parsons. Meanwhile one million women and one million men will approach new relationships in ways which will differ as a result of the experience. Our survey (see Chapter 8) seems to show that the men will approach women with more sexual interest but with far less trust. Perhaps these less trusting attitudes will also affect other dealings in life—negotiations at work, other social relationships and so on.

At some point, when the proportion of divorced people reaches a certain level, the demographic and financial effects on the pattern of economic demand may well be seen as significant. The permeation through society of new attitudes held by a sizeable minority of people as a result of a chastening marital experience and perhaps too as a result of reading feminist work may well affect the overall tenor of social relations. There may be many more guarded and disillusioned adults and many more anti-authoritarian children. Certainly many joint domestic financial arrangements will have been taken apart and many mortgages foreclosed. Equally the cost to the public sector of counselling and guidance before the break-up, legal proceedings at the time, and expenditure on state benefits plus medical and psychological care for many of those damaged will be seen to be an unreasonably heavy drain on the state's resources, especially in the current deep recession. In all these ways a rapidly rising divorce rate may well work to destabilise society, economically, politically and socially in the manner hinted at, but hardly ever specifically explored, by most of the authors quoted in these two chapters. If the divorce rate continues to rise at the current rate we would see upwards of five million new divorces in the 1980s. If it is correct that there is a link between the stability of the family and the stability of society, as commentators on both the 'left' and the 'right' unhesitatingly assert, the effects of this can hardly be left unconsidered. As authors, we make no comment at this time either for or against greater liberalisation of the divorce laws. We merely point out that the issue now has perhaps unprecedented societal, as well as personal, ramifications.

Chapter 3
Some Basic Information

Number of Divorces

Before 1939 there were never more than 10,000 divorces per year. High cost, legal difficulties and social stigma were among the factors limiting divorce as a form of marriage termination. There were, and of course still are, various other means of effectively ending a marriage such as obtaining a separation order from a magistrates' court. It is, in fact, only since the Second World War that divorce has become the most common means of terminating a marriage.

Major wars lead to social upheavals and to an acceleration in certain long term trends in society. The Second World War provided a good example of this in the field of divorce. By 1947 the number of divorces had increased to around 60,000, over six times the pre-war average (Leete, 1979). This partly reflected a realistic adjustment following the hiatus caused by enforced separations during the war. During the 1950s, numbers fell and by 1960 the annual number was back down to 24,000.

During the 1960s, however, a long-term upward trend became evident and divorces increased steadily at the rate of about 9 per cent per year so that by 1970 the number had reached 58,000. In 1971 the 1969 Divorce Law Reform Act became effective and a sharp increase occurred to 119,000 in 1972. Although this rapid doubling of divorces represented a 'backlog' effect following the changes in the law, it has since become clear that the underlying trend is still upward. By 1976 the number had reached 127,000 and in 1980 it was 148,000 (Central Statistical Office, 1981). The upward trend was also reflected in the number of redivorces which rose from 9 per cent of all divorces to nearly 16 per cent in the sixteen year period 1964–80.

Because of changes in demographic structure and other factors, it is more accurate to discuss changes in *divorce rates* (i.e. the number of divorces per year per 1000 married people) than simply in the total number of divorces. This annual rate increased from 2.1 per 1000 in 1961 to 12.0 in 1980. Subdividing the population into different age groups, the peak 'risk' age bracket is 25 to 29. In 1976, for every 1000 married men of this age, 21.3 became divorced and for every 1000 married women 20.5. *Growth* in these divorce rates has been most evident in the under-25 age group, both for men and for women, although there has also been a big increase, since the 1969 Act took effect, in the divorce rate for people over 50. No doubt this too reflects a backlog of marriages which had, in real terms, broken down previously.

Length of Marriage

In considering the average length of marriages that end in divorce, and the existence or otherwise of such phenomena as the 'seven-year itch', it must be remembered that legal termination may well come several, or even many, years after the marriage has effectively ended. The following figures therefore consistently over-state the real duration of marriages that are terminated. Between 1964 and 1976 there was no clear change in the average length of marriages ending in divorce, in fact the average length of ten to twelve years hardly changed over this time. Nor, contrary to generally held belief, were there any peak periods in the life of marriages at which divorces were most frequent (see Figure 1).

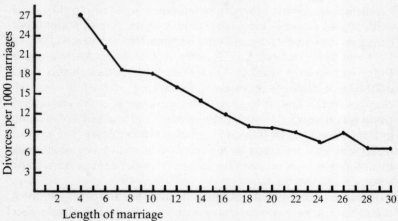

Fig. 1 Divorce rate and length of marriage, 1976.
Source: Leete, 1979.

To some extent the high four-year rate probably reflects a backlog effect since it is extremely difficult to obtain a divorce in the first three years of marriage. Even so there has been some increase in the incidence of divorce during the early years of marriage. In 1971 13 per cent of divorces had occurred within the first four years of marriage whereas by 1979 this proportion had risen to 19 per cent.

The Effects of Marrying Young

The younger the partners the more probable that the marriage will end in divorce. This applies for all marriages, whether shortlived or longer lasting. For example, we have seen from Figure 1 that in 1976, twenty-seven of every 1000 marriages that had lasted four years ended in divorce. In those cases where the bride had been aged under 20 when married the rate was forty-six divorces per 1000 marriages, nearly double the risk. Where the bride had been between 25 and 29, the rate was only eighteen divorces per 1000 marriages. In other words marrying in the late 20s rather than in one's teens seems to reduce the chances of an early divorce about two-and-a-half times. In fact 80 per cent of divorces occur in marriages where the wife was under 25 when marrying. Also, on the whole, there is a somewhat greater chance of a marriage ending in divorce if the woman is *older* than the man rather than the same age or younger. Over recent years there has been a steady fall in the age at which divorce occurs. In 1964 the median age of men obtaining a divorce was 37.2 years but by 1976 this had fallen to 35.6. For women the figures for the same two years were 34.2 and 33.1.

Children of Divorcing Couples

Divorce tends to be a much more painful and complicated affair, both emotionally and financially, if children are involved. In this context 'children' are now defined as those under the age of sixteen when the petition was filed. Before 1974 children of the marriage of whatever age were included in the statistics, so some problems arise in making comparisons over time. To complicate matters, before 1970 Court Clerks recorded only the number of children involved in a divorce case and not their ages, so no detailed comparisons can be made except from 1970. Nevertheless the increase in the number of children affected by divorce, even since this date, is very striking:

Year of divorce	Number of couples	Number of children under 16
1970	58,200	71,300
1979	138,000	155,000

Source: *Social Trends*.

In 1976, of the 78,000 divorcing couples who had at least one child under 16, 64 per cent had only school-age children, 19 per cent had only children under school-age, and the remaining 17 per cent had some pre-school and some school age. Thus in that year it seems likely that over two-thirds of the children involved in divorce cases were already attending school. But in 36 per cent of cases, at least one child of the couple was of pre-school age. In these cases very considerable problems are likely to arise for the parent granted custody as she or he seeks to maintain a home and an income despite the needs of at least one pre-school child. Naturally in times of economic recession such problems are greatly exacerbated due to the contraction of employment, especially part-time employment. At the same time cutbacks in public expenditure result in the removal of various support services such as nursery schools, playgroups and crêches.

One-Parent Families

Any divorce involving children leads to the creation of a one-parent family unless and until the custodial parent remarries. Even if the parents remain on friendly terms, live close to each other and both keep in close touch with the children, many difficulties are inherent in this arrangement. The number of such households was estimated at 367,000 in 1961, 570,000 in 1971, 750,000 in 1976, and 900,000 in 1981 (OPCS, 1978 and Central Statistical Office, 1981). This is an increase of 245 per cent in twenty years. The vast majority of these families are headed by women. In 1971, of one-parent families with dependent children, only about 12 per cent were headed by men and the percentage appeared not to have changed by 1976.

It is reasonable to ask whether there is any evidence that the presence (or absence) of children affects the likelihood of a divorce occurring. To put it a slightly different way, do couples stay together 'because of the children'? The statistical information available sheds very little light on this question. On the one hand, as was shown earlier, the incidence of divorce does not 'peak' at any particular period after marriage so there is no sign of a tendency to obtain a divorce once the care of dependent children had been completed (fifteen to twenty years after marriage on average?). On the other hand, at all durations of marriage, childless couples show a greater propensity to get divorced than do those with children. This can be interpreted in various ways, for example it may be true that in some cases an inability to have children is actually a contributory factor in the divorce. None of this evidence is anything more than indicative of further questions that would need to be separately researched.

Remarriage

Partly, no doubt, because of the growing incidence of divorce, and thus of a population eligible to remarry, there has been a striking growth in second (and subsequent) marriages. It has been estimated that about half of those getting divorced in any given year remarry within five years. Whereas in 1961, only 14 per cent of all marriages involved a partner who had previously been married, this proportion rose to 20 per cent in 1971 and 34 per cent in 1979 (Central Statistical Office, 1981). Given that at least one of the partners to the new marriage is very likely to have children by a previous marriage, there has clearly been a rapid recent increase in step-parenting.

Grounds for Divorce

Any study of changes in the pattern of grounds for divorce is complicated by changes in the law which became effective in 1971 and which introduced new grounds for divorce, such as two years or five years separation. Nevertheless two reasons still stand out as predominant grounds: adultery (in the case of petitions by husband) and cruelty (where the wife petitions). This is shown in the form of percentages in the table overleaf.

  Several points stand out. Cruelty by the other partner is a

	Petition by husbands (38,300 cases or 30.6% of all divorces)	Petition by wives (87,000 cases or 69.4% of all divorces)
	(percentages)	
Adultery	40.6	24.5
Cruelty	6.6	37.9
Desertion	3.1	4.5
Two years' separation	31.9	23.1
Five years' separation	16.8	8.2
Others	1.0	1.8
	100.0	100.0

Source: Leete, 1979.

ground used overwhelmingly by women. In fact 93 per cent of the divorces granted on grounds of cruelty were sought by women and this percentage has changed very little since the early 1960s. By contrast adultery easily rates highest of the reasons cited by man. Petitions based on desertion, which in 1964 were fairly evenly balanced between the sexes, are now brought by women in three cases out of four but the separation grounds introduced by the 1969/71 legislation are used, proportionately, much more by men than women.

The Future

There are many factors affecting the incidence of divorce and predictions for the future can never be much more than projections of current trends. There has been a trend during the 1970s towards a slight increase in the average age at marrying and given the extra risk of divorce involved where the partners marry young, fewer divorces might be expected if this trend continues. But perhaps more significant are any future changes in the law and the ease and cost of obtaining a divorce. As has been argued in Chapter 2, the issue is to a considerable extent a political one since any legislation concerning divorce incorporates tacit assumptions not only about the proper economic role of women (and men) in society but also about the significance of the nuclear family as a force for social and political stability. It is also a religious issue, it being held by many that marriages are made in heaven. The views of the various churches are therefore far more significant, and more effectively propagated, in this field than in some others.

Looking back, it has been found (Leete, 1979) that of men and women born in 1926, nearly 10 per cent had experienced a divorce by the time they were 50 (i.e. in 1976). On present trends this proportion is likely to rise to 16 per cent of those born in 1936 and 28 per cent of those born in 1951; a divorce risk of greater than one in four. Projections of the 'marriage history' of those married in 1972 show that 13 per cent of the marriages are likely to be terminated within ten years, 19 per cent within fifteen years, and 27 per cent within twenty-five years. If the wife was aged under 20 on her wedding day, these projections increase to 23 per cent within ten years, 34 per cent within fifteen years and 48 per cent within twenty-five years.

Thus the final, rather sobering, conclusion of contemporary research is that up to a half of marriages contracted by teenage brides are, on present trends, likely to end in the divorce court. All these data form part of the general context in which we decided to carry out research into the effects of marital breakdown as experienced particularly by men. The methods we used to find out about the experiences and feelings of a sample of ninety-two divorced men are set out in Appendix I and the results are detailed in the five chapters that follow.

Chapter 4
The Divorce

The ninety-two divorces vary from those finalised in the few months previous to the survey to one made absolute thirty-three years ago. They therefore occurred between the years 1948 and 1981. There is, however, a strong preponderance of recent divorces in the study. Just over three-quarters had occurred within the previous five years and over nine-tenths in the decade since the new divorce law became operational in 1971.

There are several good reasons for this pattern. The number of divorces increased considerably anyway during the 1970s as shown in Chapter 3. But quite apart from this, and because the survey was carried out on those who responded to advertisements (see Appendix 1), the sample was essentially self-selective. The men most likely to respond to the various advertisements were those for whom the divorce had been a comparatively recent event. Few people divorced in the 1950s and 1960s, and possibly remarried for many years, were likely to take the trouble to complete the form. Of those who did, one made the understandable, but quite erroneous, observation that his case was probably of little interest to us since it all happened so long ago.

The length of the marriages ending in divorce varied from two years in one case to forty-one years at the other extreme. The average length of the marriages was just over eleven and a half years. Ten and eleven-year marriages were the most common and nearly one-third of the divorces had occurred after a marriage length of between seven and eleven years which, allowing for various 'lag factors', does give some credence to the notion of the 'seven-year itch'. Occupational class appeared to have no discernable affect on marriage length since all classes (except for the three retired divorcees) averaged from nine to eleven years in marriage length. The full distribution of ages at which the marriages had occurred is set out in Appendix 1. In all cases this was the husband's age since no information was collected on the age of the wife. Over 15 per cent of the marriages had been contracted by age 21 and over

53 per cent by age 25. This was in fact by far the most frequent age for marriage to occur and it accounted for sixteen of the ninety-two cases. Of the men in the sample, six had been married previously (just once in all cases) and none of these had since remarried so none of the sample had embarked upon marriage for a third time.

The Children Involved

One hundred and forty-five children were involved in the ninety-two divorces. This includes children of all ages including those classed for the purposes of this study as 'non-custodial' (i.e. over 16) as well as younger children. The breakdown of family size at the time of divorce was as shown.

Number of children per couple	Number of couples	Total number of children
0	16	0
1	23	23
2	40	80
3	11	33
4	1	4
5	1	5
		145

The average number of children per family was therefore 1.58 which, as might be expected, is considerably less than the national average. If the 'non-custodial' children are removed from the calculation, the average number of children per couple was only 1.18, a figure rather lower than might have been expected given an average marriage 'life' of about eleven years but one well in line with the national average which for 1977 divorces was 1.15 (*Social Trends*, 1980). Possibly two factors are at work here: some couples may have had difficulties starting a family or perhaps disagreements or inhibitions about doing so, or having more children, because they felt the marriage to be a less than solid one. In many cases also it was evident from comments that sexual relations between the couple had been very unsatisfactory or even absent. In fact one man commented, following ten years of marriage:

My ex-wife did not want a family and therefore did not want to have sex. She stated that if we did not indulge we could not have a family.

For other men the birth of the first child had a bad effect on sexual relations:

After our first child was born, things seemed to be going wrong. The baby for instance would sleep in the middle of our bed, sex was almost non-existent. I felt very rejected . . . I was just not there.

The average length of marriage does vary quite sharply depending upon the number of children in the family as shown below.

Number of children	Average length of marriage in years
0	5.6
1	10.4
2	12.6
3 or more	13.8

In this respect, as in many others to be discussed later, childless divorces constitute quite a separate case from those where children are involved.

Who Petitioned

In the sample the pattern of petitioning was as follows (in percentages):

Husband	40.2
Wife	50.0
Both	9.8

Compared to the national trend during the period over which most divorces in the survey occurred, there is a marked over representation of men petitioners in the survey. According to the 1982 edition of *Social Trends*, the proportion of men petitioners for selected recent years was as follows (in percentages):

1961	43
1971	40
1975	30
1980	28

The national trend towards wives as petitioners is quite clear. This was not reflected in the study sample since in the thirty-seven cases where the man petitioned the average number of years since the divorce was 5.2 years. The average length of marriage for the three petitioning groups was as follows:

Who petitioned	Average length of marriage in years
Husband	12.1
Wife	10.7
Both	8.3

These differences are unsurprising since those marriages which both parties wished to end might have been expected to last a shorter period than others.

There is a difference in the pattern of petitioning by occupational class as the following table shows:

Occupational classes	Husband	Petitioner Wife (percentages)	Both
Professional and higher skilled non-manual occupations	41	39	20
Low-skilled non-manual and all manual occupations	37	63	0

The balance of petitioning noted on a national scale is more closely reflected in the 'lower' occupational groups while petitioning by both parties was confined to the 'higher' groups. Age at marriage appears to have no significant effect on the pattern of petitioning.

It is as well to remember, when considering the pattern of petitioning, that it is by no means always the partner filing the petition who most wishes the marriage to end. One man, whose wife had started a part-time job, acquired a measure of independence by passing her driving test, and had then begun to meet other men, gave this account of how the marriage finally broke up:

After I left home, I went back and asked her for a divorce. To me it didn't feel right as she was with someone. I told her she could file, if not I would.

In fact the wife petitioned and applied for custody of the two children. Neither matter was contested by the man.

Reasons Given for the Break-up

The survey form included the question: '*Can you give a brief account of the main reasons, as you see them, why the marriage broke up?*' As might be expected, the answers varied from the very terse to the very expansive but the general impression gained was that serious thought had been given to the question and certainly everything offered by way of explanation was printable. The reasons given are shown in the table below in the order of frequency in which they were mentioned.

Reason for break-up	Number of men giving this reason
Affairs/infidelity (by either)	32
Incompatibility/impossible relationship	19
Serious sex problems	14
Poor communication/understanding	11
Wife met/wished to marry someone else	9
Arguments/problems over money	9
Wife's affinity to her mother	8
Work interfered with relationship (self or wife's work)	8
Married too early with not enough thought	8
Wife had a serious illness or disablement	8
Lack of affection/love	7
Did not share common aims	6
Differences concerning children's upbringing	5
Wife unreasonable/nagging/jealous	4
Wife wanted to work	4
Very different backgrounds	4
Husband met/wished to marry someone else	4
Violence by husband, wife or children	4
Difference in age	3
Wife seemed to change after birth of children	3
Wife's cruelty or neglect of children	3
Wife just lost all interest	2
Wife favoured her own previous children	2
Feminist ideas by wife	2
Expectations not fulfilled	1
Husband's serious illness	1
Drink problems	1
Husband felt 'used' as child producer	1
No evident reason	1
	184

This is clearly a very varied set of reasons, and on the basis of a survey of this kind it is impossible to sort responses into watertight categories because there are various stages at which fine shades of meaning can be lost. For example, many of the 'affairs' mentioned no doubt arose as a partial result of serious sex problems which were perhaps not stated as such. It is also noteworthy that none of the respondent's mentioned 'housing difficulties' as a contributory factor although it is well established that severe housing problems place great stress on many marriages and lead directly to marriage break-up in a large number of cases. Possibly this factor would have become more apparent had the survey been addressed to women rather than men—so perhaps would have been references to the part played by feminist ideas, to the wife's attempt to gain greater economic independence and to highly anti-social behaviour such as violence and heavy drinking (all mentioned in very few cases).

Despite all these reservations, an attempt was made to sort the 184 reasons mentioned (an average of exactly two per respondent) into categories as shown below:

Nature of reason	Number of times given	
Internal to the marriage and concerning the relationship between the couple alone	71	Reasons purely internal to the marriage
Internal to the marriage but concerning the couple and their children	15	= 86 times stated
Relationship by one or both of the parties with another or others	45	Pressure from outside the marriage
Tensions related to the career (of either party) or money matters	21	= 74 times stated
Pressures from mother-in-law	8	
Reasons relating to an original inappropriate choice of partner	15	
Illness of either party	9	
	184	

The striking feature here is the extent to which the explanations offered were centred on the relationship of the pair alone. Pressures arising from work, children, money problems, mothers-in-law, etc. were all far less significant, at least in terms of frequency of mention, than the sheer erosion and final failure of the relationship between the two people in question. Affairs or infidelity were referred to by nearly half the sample but there is no means of knowing, short of extensive personal interviewing, the extent to which other people instigated or hastened the failure of the marriage or were turned to for consolation following acceptance by one or both of the couple that the marriage was not satisfactory to them.

From the comments made by various men it is possible to gain a clear insight into how things went wrong. Many felt they had married too early and with too little thought (ages at marriage are given in brackets after the comments):

I entered marriage without even thinking about it. It was part of the cultural norm for me.

(25 years)

I was emotionally unprepared for marriage and, in fact, did not take it seriously.

(23 years)

Neither knew how to handle relationships, neither of us had any concept of non-possessing, non-property-owning relationships.

(25 years)

Other felt sexually unprepared:

Married too early and with insufficient sexual experience.

(25 years)

Both virgins at marriage (Church)

(28 years)

Others again described the growing incompatibilities:

We grew apart in intellectual needs etc. The marriage was based on the transient needs of growing up.

(23 years)

We saw and understood the world in rather different ways. This wasn't so clear or so important at first but over time it came to feel quite untenable. In particular we failed to agree, or negotiate, the differences in our feelings about having children.

(25 years)

It is noteworthy, and perhaps slightly puzzling, that all these references to a lack of maturity when embarking on marriage are made by men who married around their mid-twenties, not by those who married as teenagers.

Some men in the sample were left with a distinct sense of having been *used* in the marriage:

She didn't believe in the marriage (or Marriage) from the start. She needed me for a time only. Highly intelligent, active, gregarious, she had needs and aims that included me out.

She just used me to obtain security, to bear and bring up young children to school age after which she sought to return to independence. There was nothing left for her to take from the relationship. . . .

The man who made the last comment was divorced by his wife at the age of forty-one after a nine-year marriage. He contested the petition and then, unsuccessfully, the issue of custody. His two young children now live four miles away and he sees them weekly. He considers that he needs to devote so much time to disputes about access that his small business has been badly affected.

As a final question about the divorce, each respondent was also asked: '*Was there any particular event or action that made you feel that divorce was inevitable; if so, what was it?*' As a subsidiary, the question was put: '. . . *if so, how many years before the actual divorce was this?*' In sixty-seven of the ninety-two cases a 'trigger' event was stated, as shown below.

Reason	Number of times given
Wife left or intended to leave	15
Wife had affair or new relationship	12
Husband had affair or new relationship	7
Increasing rows or violence	6
Husband left	6
Basic change in wife's behaviour	4
Husband told to leave	2
Both moved out or separated	2
Wife stole money	2
Husband's drink problem	2
Wife took the children away	1
Wife had abortions against husband's wishes	1
Caught wife in bed with another man	1
Wife's attempted suicide	1
Another woman's intervention with the child	1
Trial separation	1
Wife's antipathy to husband's family	1
Discovery of love letter to wife	1
Suggestion of son or daughter	1
	67

These can be loosely categorised as follows:

Nature of action	Number of times given
Wife-initiated actions	40
Husband-initiated actions	15
Mutually initiated actions	10
Events external to the couple	2
	67

Two points are worth noting. First, whereas the balance of those petitioning was fairly even in the sample (thirty-seven men to forty-six women) the husbands' accounts of the events that made divorce inevitable, which cannot of course be regarded as any kind of objective truth, are much more heavily weighted towards events initiated by the wife (forty to fifteen). The second point is that whereas external factors played a strong part in the set of reasons given for the failure of the marriage, the 'trigger' events that brought matters to a head were virtually all initiated by the couple themselves.

The 'dead period' of the marriage, that is the period between the husband's acceptance that divorce was inevitable and the granting of the decree, was on the whole surprisingly short (given the emotional, financial and legal hurdles that have to be overcome to terminate a marriage):

'Dead period' (in years)	Number of cases
1	15
2	20
3	12
4 to 12	7
	54

It is reasonable to assume that this brevity (for the majority) of the transitional period from married to single status owes a great deal to the change in the law that became effective in 1971. Some would see this as on balance a positive result of the change. Others would argue that the comparative liberality of present law had allowed a large proportion of people to rush too quickly into a divorce and that, given better conciliatory services and more testing legal procedures, the period here referred to as a 'dead period' could in some cases have been a 'revival period'.

Whatever the respective merits of these two views, the evidence from the survey is that few of those questioned appeared to feel that it was worth a fight to save the marriage or to challenge the petitioner's version of events. In only nine of the ninety-two cases was the petition contested. No doubt in other cases one or other party might have felt that it *should* have been but were advised by their lawyer that there was little point in doing so since the task of the court is now to ascertain whether or not the marriage has irrevocably broken down and not to judge between different versions of events in order to allocate degrees of blame. Occupational class had no effect on the likelihood of contesting the case but the sex of the petitioner had a clear effect; in eight of the nine contested cases the wife was the petitioner and the husband the contester.

Custody of the Children

In sixty-six of the ninety-two divorces (72 per cent) one or more children of custodial age were involved. The 1980 edition of *Social Trends* records that the national percentage of such divorces was 60 per cent. The issue of custody was contested in twenty-three cases and left uncontested in the remaining forty-three. The men involved in the contested cases had no particularly social or economic characteristics. It is important to note that there is much evidence from observations on a number of survey forms that considerably more than twenty-three men *would have* contested the custody issue had the lawyer not advised against such a course since in his (or her) view there would be little chance of winning. Other lawyers, as is well known, simply will not agree to contest custody proceedings. Apart from these factors, which no doubt have a powerful effect at the time, there was at least one man in the sample who simply did not know (and presumably had not been told) that the issue of custody could be contested at all. All this no doubt helps to explain the high levels of resentment still felt by many men in the survey— an issue to be discussed at the end of the chapter.

The overall pattern of custody decisions is shown on the next page. We tried to find out what factors seem to have affected this

	Number of cases	Percentage of cases
Custody to wife	45	68
Custody to husband	8	12
Joint custody	8	12
Some other arrangement	5	8
	66	100

outcome. The average age of the children whose custody was awarded to the husband was notably higher than for those where custody went to the wife—over 14 years of age as against 11. Similarly occupational class seems to make a difference since six of the eight cases of custody to the father were to men in non-manual occupations. Of these eight cases only one concerned a single child, four involved a two-child family, one a three-child family and, perhaps surprisingly, custody of the two largest families in the sample (one of four children and one of five) went to the father following uncontested cases. Possibly a woman would not find this surprising. The identity of the petitioner relates to the custody outcome as shown:

Petitioner	Custody to husband, both jointly or 'other'	Custody to wife solely
Husband	12	12
Wife	6	31

Who Moved Out

The break-up of a marriage entails the generation of two households instead of one. One or other of the partners, or both, have to seek accommodation elsewhere. The pattern in our sample was as follows:

Husband moved out	40	
Wife moved out	38	
Both moved out	12	
Both still in same house	1	(very recently divorced)
Question not answered	1	
	92	

It should perhaps be noted in passing that with the rapid rise in home-ownership in recent decades (from 42 per cent in 1960 to 55 per cent in 1980) more and more divorce cases require arbitration about the current use, and the eventual division of the realised value, of a house. In view of the occupational pattern of the sample, these complications probably affect the vast majority of cases in the survey. It is impossible to say, from the evidence available, just how the capacity or otherwise to support a mortgage as a single parent affects the pattern of who moves and who stays in the matrimonial home following a divorce but the 'normal' pattern of wife plus children staying put and husband seeking new accommodation is only partly supported by the survey findings.

The pattern of moving out was not particularly affected by the length of the marriage, the age at divorce or the occupational class of the husband. It did, however, seem to be related to the identity of the petitioner in the following way:

Petitioner	Husband moved out	Wife moved out
Husband	11	20
Wife	26	14

Thus in the large majority of cases it was the petitioner who remained in the matrimonial home. The pattern also depended on whether or not there were children. For childless couples the normal pattern was for the wife, or both, to move whereas for couples with children there was a clear, but not overwhelming, tendency for the husband to find a place elsewhere. This was quite clearly related to the custody decision since in six of the eight cases where the *man* was awarded custody he stayed in the matrimonial home whereas in the cases where the *wife* was awarded custody, moves by the man exceeded those by the woman in the ratio of two to one.

How much Anger Remains?

The issue of the break-up was finally approached from the point of view of the amount of anger still evident in the men's accounts of what had happened. The observations of each respondent were arranged on a scale of 1 to 5 using the following general criteria:

1 { an accepting, highly rationalised, account of the marriage failure, ascribing roughly equal shares of blame to both parties and implying or stating in some way that the break-up happened for the best;

2 { accounts giving an impression intermediate
3 { between these two extremes in ascending order
4 { of anger, etc;

5 { an unaccepting, angry account, placing blame exclusively on the ex-wife, or other party, and implying or stating in some way that the break-up has been a highly damaging event.

The scoring was carried out independently by two of the researchers with an 80–85 per cent degree of agreement and cases of disagreement were adjudicated by the third researcher. The distribution of scores for each of the ninety-two cases was as follows:

		Number of men
1	highly accepting and well rationalised	6
2	less so	9
3	an intermediate position	26
4	fairly hostile	18
5	very unaccepting and angry	33
		92

Clearly the men in the sample, taken as a whole, were still feeling a lot of anger, hurt and blame towards their former wives since fifty-one were on the 'angry' side of the intermediate position as against only fifteen on the more accepting side.

We tried to find some explanation of the variation in strength of feeling by comparing the pattern of answers with all factors that might possibly shed some light. It seemed reasonable to expect that the passing of time might lead to a reduction in the amount of anger about the break-up. This is borne out, but not to a consistent extent, by calculating the average number of years since the divorce for each of the five groups as is indicated on the following page.

The length of the marriage seemed to have little bearing on the amount of anger still felt; this value varied fairly closely around eleven years (the average for the entire sample). Several other

	Feelings concerning marriage break-up	Average years since divorce
1	accepting and rational	5.0
2		4.0
3		3.9
4		6.1
5	non-accepting and angry	3.3

factors, however, do seem to have significance. There was a noticeable tendency for older divorcees to carry somewhat angrier feelings. The average age at divorce of the least angry group was 35.0, of the intermediate group 36.6 and of the most angry group 39.3. Occupational class also had some effect. All the 'most accepting' group and nearly 80 per cent of the 'less so' group fell in the non-manual occupations (these occupations comprised about 69 per cent of the entire sample) whereas on average much higher levels of anger still survived among those with manual occupations.

Issues concerning children appear to affect the strength of feeling in a number of different ways. Fathers feel angry about the break-up far more often than non-fathers:

Level of anger about break-up	Fathers	Non- fathers
Low or fairly low (groups 1 and 2)	9	6
High or fairly high (groups 4 and 5)	46	5

Similarly the custody outcome affects the issue. All the eight men who were granted sole custody and six of the eight granted joint custody hold feelings that vary from intermediate to very angry concerning the break-up. This weight of antagonistic feeling is much less strikingly reflected where the wife has sole custody. The same trend is evident in contests about custody. Twenty-three cases of contested custody occurred (eight of which ended with the husband as sole legal custodian). In all these twenty-three men the level of anger still held is intermediate or worse whereas eighteen of the forty-three men not contesting custody hold from intermediate to very accepting views of the marriage failure. There is thus no evidence that contesting, and/or winning, a custody case, or being granted uncontested custody, softens the feelings of anger towards the ex-wife. All the evidence points in the contrary direction.

As might be expected, there is a strong relationship between the level of anger still felt and the ease of relationship with the ex-wife concerning access in those cases where she has custody of the children. It will be shown in Chapter 7 that the ease of this relationship very much affects frequency of contact between non-custodial father and children so the matter is of considerable importance. The relationship is as follows:

Feelings concerning marriage break-up		Percentage of cases where access relationships with the ex-wife are middling or better
1	accepting and rational	100
2		75
3		29
4		40
5	non-accepting and angry	8

Another relationship to be examined was that between the anger level felt and the attitude, or behaviour, towards the ex-wife's new partner (if any). It was found that on the whole the more resentment felt about the break-up the more hostile the feelings towards the new partner. This too must be a factor affecting the ease of maintaining a close relationship between a father and his children where the ex-wife has custody and a new partner is living with her. There is also a connection between the strength of the anger felt about the break-up and the man's subsequent readiness to remarry. Of the men who felt fully accepting, or fairly accepting, of the break-up of the previous marriage, 40 per cent have remarried whereas of the rest only 26 per cent have remarried. Of the most angry group of all, only 18 per cent have remarried. This is not to say that there is any causal link between the two factors—it could well be that some other factor in the individual's personality makes it both difficult for him to come to terms with what has happened and, at the same time, reluctant or unable to embark on another attempt at marriage.

It was felt, on the whole, that this attempt to scale the residual feelings of anger and blame, and to compare it with other factors, yielded some worthwhile results. Clearly the presence or absence of children in the marriage affects the issue and, in turn, the strength of anger still felt will be seen in Chapter 7 to affect the ease of the post-divorce father/child relationship in measurable ways. For these reasons it seems that every effort should be made to minimise the anger that is probably present to some degree in every case of marriage break-up. We make some suggestions about this in the final chapter of the book.

Chapter 5
Sources of Help and Support

In our society there is no one specialist agency responsible for providing help for divorcing couples. There is a variety of agencies which offer help with specific difficulties resulting from divorce but no one body has overall responsibility for offering help to divorcees. Many of the services are of a voluntary nature and are not uniformly available throughout the country. Family life in general and marriage in particular remain private areas which lie outside the direct concern of the state and thus when difficulties arise in these areas many couples do not know where to seek help, support and advice. There is a general assumption that divorcing couples automatically turn to their family and friends and that somehow in the great majority of instances difficulties are resolved in private without recourse to outside intervention. Whilst we acknowledge that this rough and ready system works well for some we were concerned to find out in more detail what sources divorced men turned to for help and support and how they assessed the help and support they received.

In deciding to investigate this area we were aware that helpfulness is a difficult term to define since it encompasses a wide range of factors and experiences which include:

— the extent of the crisis and the degree of urgency at the point of seeking help;
— emotional state;
— previous experiences of the person or agency from whom help is sought;
— what kind of special help is required;
— how specifically the problem is presented;
— the timing and context of seeking help;
— the availability of the help and support;
— the quality of the help offered.

Moreover we acknowledged the view expressed in *Marriage Matters* that some problems remain intractable and that 'when all that can be done has been done, there will remain a hard core of misery, irremovable indeed' (Working Party, 1979).

Despite these complications in defining helpfulness we decided to ask each man to indicate the people and agencies he had turned to for help or advice and to assess, on the basis of the replies to our survey question, how helpful each source of assistance had been. To do this we devised a simple scoring system explained in detail in Appendix 2, which takes account of the *degree* of help received from the various sources. The highest (most helpful) score noted for any particular source of help was 1.76 and the lowest was 0.01. The average of all the scores was 1.03.

The thirteen possible sources of help we identified on the survey form have been arranged into three broad groups, the first of which includes two separate categories so that, in all, four main types of help are identified:

Informal help:

Family and kin—these include divorcees' parents, brothers and sisters, and in-laws.

Friends—these include the divorcees' own friends, any joint friends of the pre-divorced couple, and others including strangers, a bank manager, other children and relatives, and friends of new partners.

Semi-formal help:

Work and community contacts—these include employers, workmates and colleagues, neighbours and vicars.

Formal help:

Agencies and professionals—these include those agencies and professionals with a specific function to help with marital problems as well as doctors, lawyers and other agencies whom divorcees approached.

Family and Kin

The three sources in this group were assessed as shown in the table below.

It was clear that the great majority of those who approached their own parents and siblings found them very helpful. It was noticeable

	Percentage of men approaching this source	Average 'helping score'
Own parents	61	1.61
Own brothers and sisters	60	1.69
In-laws	48	0.14

that only sixteen of the total sample obtained any help at all from in-laws and of those who approached them 41 per cent assessed their experience as 'definitely unhelpful'. This is perhaps not surprising as it reflects the difficult position facing in-laws in apportioning their resources and loyalties between their own daughter and their former son-in-law. If it is assumed that the divorcing wives had approached their *own* parents, brothers and sisters in the same proportion as the husbands in our sample had approached them, it is unlikely that these members of the ex-wife's family would have had much spare capacity for helping their son-in-law even if they felt it appropriate. One man in interview described how he had approached his parents-in-law to help sort out the difficulties. Initially they had been helpful, but as the conflicts over money and the children developed, they withdrew. He accepted this as a natural reaction. Another man, by contrast, had found his brother-in-law and wife helpful throughout with practical matters and general support.

Friends

In this category the position was as follows:

	Percentage of men approaching this source	Average 'helping score'
Own friends	71	1.65
Joint friends	63	0.95
Other individuals	7	(not scored)

The percentage of those approaching either their own friends or joint friends of the marriage partners was even higher than for those who approached their own family and it can be seen that there was a high degree of satisfaction with the help and advice received. Of the sixty-five who approached their own friends, thirty-five found them very helpful or extremely helpful and only one definitely unhelpful. Of those who approached joint friends, thirty-seven assessed the reaction as helpful and only three assessed it as definitely unhelpful. It would seem, as might be expected, that joint friends do not experience the same level of divided loyalties and pressures as do in-laws in giving help and advice.

Although the numbers are small it is also noticeable that those who approached other people such as strangers and casual contacts with whom there was neither friendship nor family ties found them invariably helpful, with five describing them as extremely helpful. Evidently some people find it easier to disclose their problems to someone who knows little or nothing about the context and the participants involved. One man who found his bank manager very helpful thought it was because there were concrete issues to do with the divorce settlement to sort out so that their meeting had a built-in 'agenda'.

Work and Community Contacts

Four separate sources were identified here, as follows:

	Percentage of men approaching this source	Average 'helping score'
Workmates and colleagues	51	1.51
Employers	40	1.41
Neighbours	34	0.81
Vicars	18	0.88

It can be seen that the percentage of those who approached each of the sources in this category is lower than for those who approached family and friends. Vicars were approached by only a small number of men and this may reflect the lack of recognition that the church has a part to play at times of marital break-up. We find this both saddening and ironic in view of the major role played by the various churches, both historically and in the present day, in defining the nature of the marriage bond (see Chapter 1) and in actually marrying the couples.

The great majority of workmates and colleagues approached were experienced as helpful, as were employers, with only five men in all experiencing them as definitely unhelpful. We were surprised that employers provided such a significant and valued source of help and advice to many of the respondents. We had anticipated that many men would not want to disclose confidential information about their marriage breakdown to their employers in case it affected their career prospects and status in the organisation. If there is still a degree of social stigma attached to being divorced we had expected that it might be found at the work place. We have of course no way of knowing what effects such disclosures may have on the men's future career, but in the short run many employers were a significant source of help. With regard to workmates and colleagues, it is less surprising that of those approached the great majority were found to be helpful. The workplace is clearly an important source of help and advice and we suggest in Chapter 9 that more thought needs to be given to building on this base when developing counselling and advice services for divorced men.

The significance and value of neighbours as measured by the index is perhaps less surprising. Many of the men had moved out of the family home after the break-up and had automatically lost this possible source of help. But those who remained in the matrimonial home had clearly derived much support from their neighbours. Certainly where there are children involved there would be natural links through their relationships in the neighbourhood, at school and through other local activities and clubs.

Agencies and Professionals

The questionnaire sought information about the help offered by doctors, solicitors, social workers and marriage guidance counsellors. A further twenty-one sources of formal help were added by those completing the forms and for the analysis these were divided into two categories 'other voluntary services' and 'other state services'. *

---

* The other state services included the Probation Service, schools, Education Department, and the other voluntary services included the Institute of Marital Studies, psychoanalysts, psychotherapists, the Tavistock Institute, the Samaritans, Citizens Advice Bureaux, Families Need Fathers and the Campaign for Justice in Divorce.

The rates of referral and level of help received were as follows:

	Percentage of men approaching this source	Average 'helping score'
Solicitors	68	0.98
Doctors	51	0.85
Marriage guidance	32	0.38
Social workers	29	0.01
Other voluntary services	20	1.76
Other state services	3	0.75

Doctors figured as important sources of help and advice for about half the men even though they do not have a specific role in helping with divorce difficulties. In view of the very high incidence of men in our sample who had both physical and mental health conditions following divorce (see Chapter 7), it is likely that many of the men went to the surgery presenting physical symptoms rather than to discuss the break-up of their marriage. One man at interview, for example, described how he had visited his doctor because he thought he was about to have a heart attack. The other organisations whose functions are more specifically geared to deal with family and marital difficulties were, somewhat surprisingly, approached much less often. Marriage Guidance in particular with its long tradition of marital counselling was approached by only 32 per cent of the men and was found, on the whole, to be fairly unhelpful. With regard to social workers, the questionnaire did not ask respondents to differentiate among the many organisations who employ them. The very low score for helpfulness therefore reflects the help, or more frequently lack of it, obtained from all those described by our respondents as social workers.

These results seem to call for some interpretation. Doctors and lawyers of course provide well known and well established professional services and are perhaps seen as more readily available and accessible than are social workers and Marriage Guidance. It may be easier to approach doctors and lawyers for the very reason that they are *not* seen as specifically geared to helping only with divorce problems. Probably also in the case of doctors, and sometimes lawyers, there may already be a relationship in existence prior to the break-up. Where this is so it may be easier to approach them than take the initiative to visit a 'stranger' who knows little about the background and the personalities involved, and whose functions may not be at all clear in the minds of the men seeking help.

With regard to social workers, we are aware that often they become involved in marital problems only when there are disputes about custody, access and the care of children, where there are serious mental health problems which might lead to hospitalisation, or in cases of homelessness. Each of these areas is emotionally charged, especially following a break-up. So when a dispute cannot be resolved by the parties or by the solicitor, or when the doctor considers the difficulties to be outside his or her range of skills, it often happens that the divorcing man is referred, or directed, to a social worker for help. Such referrals can alter the basis of the relationship with the social worker from a voluntarily sought contact to one where there is some degree of obligation and pressure. This may have an adverse effect on the subsequent relationship.

Finally the very high scores for the voluntary organisations came about because of the extremely helpful rating given by three of the eight men who approached Families Need Fathers and the Campaign for Justice in Divorce and the two who approached the Samaritans and the Tavistock Institute. In sharp contrast, the lower mean scores for doctors, solicitors, social workers and marriage guidance resulted partly from the large number of men who rated their help and advice as definitely unhelpful.

Summary

The scorings for all sources of help can now be collated in the order of their assessed helpfulness (see Appendix 2). To the information already given, the table below adds the percentage of 'extremely helpful' and 'definitely unhelpful' responses obtained from each.

It is evident that voluntary organisations and services score very highly, even though the number of men approaching them is very small compared with all the other sources. Two such organisations are The Campaign for Justice in Divorce and Families Need Fathers. Both are pressure groups for reform in divorce law and practice as well as agencies for helping individuals through their divorce and post-divorce problems. All the men who approached them valued their help and concern and in some instances their willingness to take initiatives on their behalf. The significance of voluntary organ-

	Average 'helping score'	Percentage of men approaching this source	Percentage of extremely help-ful responses	Percentage of definitely unhelpful responses
Other voluntary services	1.76	20	36	5
Brothers and sisters	1.69	60	36	7
Own friends	1.65	71	23	2
Own parents	1.61	61	29	4
Workmates and colleagues	1.51	51	21	2
Employers	1.41	40	19	6
Solicitors	0.98	68	11	16
Joint friends	0.95	63	10	5
Vicars	0.88	18	12	18
Doctors	0.85	51	11	13
Neighbours	0.81	34	6	3
Other state services	0.75	3	0	33
Marriage guidance	0.38	32	7	28
In-laws	0.14	48	7	41
Social workers	0.01	29	7	44

isations and private counsellors and therapists (as opposed to, for example, doctors) may lie in the greater ease felt by those who seek help in unloading their problems towards people who have not only expertise but often more time available to deal with them. It may also reflect the fact that making an appointment to see a specialist helper involves a certain amount of preparation and pre-thought which may well increase the motivation to use what help is offered. The irony is that only seventeen men found their way to seeking help from the various voluntary and private sources which are available. Probably most men had not heard of their existence.

It is equally striking that all other sources of help and advice falling above the overall average score of 1.03 are ones we have grouped as informal or semi-formal. Friends, parents, brothers and sisters, and work colleagues are all very significant sources of help in terms not only of the readiness of men to approach them but also in the high proportion of extremely helpful responses obtained. By contrast, doctors, lawyers, vicars and other formal services, although in some cases approached by a large proportion of our sample, were found to be less helpful and supportive. And the final conclusion to emerge from our material is that the social services generally, including services specifically set up to assist in the general field of family welfare, were found to be of least assistance with definitely unhelpful responses heavily outweighing helpful ones.

Difficulties in Seeking Help

It is clear that family, kin, friends and work relationships are extremely important sources of help for the great majority of our divorced men. This is not altogether surprising; family and friendship networks are major institutions in our social structure and can be expected to provide help at times of crisis. But problems arise for divorced men when their family, friendship or work networks are either non-existent, limited in size or fragile and are thus unable to provide the appropriate kind of help. As the Working Party on Marriage Guidance (1979) says 'dealing with marital problems is particularly stressful, time-consuming and emotionally demanding'. It would not be surprising if many friends, workmates and family members felt unable to cope with these pressures, particularly over long periods of time—however willing they may be. Moreover, as the Working Party comments, when someone offers help, 'he will have to listen to accounts of marriage problems which may be all too close for his own comfort'.

When the stress and strains of the break-up cannot be adequately met by the informal support networks the divorcee is faced with the problem: where to go and whom to approach. Since doctors are consulted about a wide range of anxiety and stress-based problems it is likely that those who decide to seek further help will look to their doctor as a first point of reference. In a study by Chester of divorced women (1971) over 90 per cent of them approached their doctors for help at the time of the break-up. Our sample suggests that considerably fewer men approach their doctors and the same reluctance to seek help seems to limit their contact with other formal support systems. Why might this be? The Working Party (1979) in discussing the problems facing those who seek help with their marital problems, stress the difficulties of seeking help:

. . . he must be inclined, determined or even desperate to seek advice. He needs information about how to locate the agency, but more especially he requires initiative and courage . . . 'crossing the threshold' . . . can be a natural deterrent to those who are apprehensive, overwrought or both.

Furthermore they underline the fear of the unknown and the uncertainty of the outcome of discussing their difficulties—many may
prefer to live with their own certainty, however painful or uncomfortable it is. In view of the very small number who approached
people and agencies outside the better known ones, the problem for
most of our sample seems to have been ignorance and a lack of
information about what is available. It was noticeable, amongst
those who approached Families Need Fathers, that there is a chain
link effect, with existing members recruiting other men. Such an
informal structure seems to have a lot of merit and ways need to be
found to extend the chain link effect.

We consider, however, that despite the generally invaluable
assistance from family, friends, employers and work colleagues
there is inadequate provision, or inadequate knowledge of the
provision, available to help men with post-divorce problems. The
Working Party (1979) believes the present array of doors on which
to knock should continue to be available and that the best way
forward 'is to improve the service provided behind each door so that
the client, on entering, will not be ill-served'. Whilst we support this
view, we consider that much more thought needs to be given to
providing the key referral people, particularly doctors and lawyers,
with more information about what is available. Furthermore we feel
that better informal networks should be established between all
those involved to bridge the apparent gap between the informal and
formal support systems. Finally, we would include the workplace as
another important point of referral and we return to this point in our
'Afterthoughts'.

Chapter 6
The Solicitor

All societies are faced with what to do when marriages break up and when one or both parties want to remarry. On the one hand there is usually a concern to reaffirm the importance of marriage as a social institution and family life as the basis for bringing up children; on the other there is increasing recognition that unhappy marriages and acrimonious family life may not always be conducive to such ends. Balancing these two conflicting positions poses serious problems. In practice the legal system is used to arbitrate between them when individual cases come to court. Inevitably in attempting to promote family life in general, and at the same time allow for individual deviations from the norm, there will be many inconsistencies and anomalies. In Britain the current controversy over the divorce laws centres on the relevance of *the adversarial system of justice* for settling divorce disputes and accompanying problems. Several recent commentators have made this point very clearly. Trevor Berry of Families Need Fathers described this system as 'combative, antagonistic and encourages a good fight. Cases are described as "x" versus "x" . . . precisely the worst point from which to start' (article in *The Times*, 7 January 1981). Similarly another commentator has argued that an 'amicable modus vivendi is less likely to be reached where the system pits husband and wife against each other, with one ultimately emerging the winner and the other the loser' (Dyer, article in *The Times*, 6 August 1980).

In the light of the general disquiet about the adversarial system we decided to examine the role of the solicitor. He or she is usually the first point of contact with the legal system for most people seeking a divorce, and it is the solicitor's professional advice, manner and attitudes which can be influential in what happens thereafter as the case goes through the legal machinery to its conclusion. In the previous chapter we reported how sixty-three men (68 per cent of our sample) evaluated the assistance they received from solicitors. On the whole they were found to be just slightly less helpful than the average of all sources of help and advice approached.

When we examined all the ninety-two responses we discovered that a further thirteen men approached solicitors for help and advice although they did not specifically rate them for helpfulness. However, as each of these men commented on the ways in which their solicitor had been helpful or unhelpful, their comments were evaluated and incorporated into the analysis that follows. The evaluation made by all seventy-six men who used or approached a solicitor was:

	Number of men
Extremely helpful	8
Very helpful	14
Fairly helpful	32
No help	11
Definitely unhelpful	11
	76

Amongst the remaining sixteen men, eleven did not use a solicitor to obtain their divorce and a further five did not mention at all whether or not they approached one.

In view of the current debate about whether solicitors are the most appropriate professional group to be involved in certain aspects of divorce counselling (because of the adversarial nature of the system) the overall assessment is reasonably positive. However it is possible, as Murch suggests, that such a positive evaluation 'may have greater significance for the light it sheds on the way divorcing clients perceive their solicitors and their relationship with them' (Murch, 1980). We decided to take up this point by exploring the main criteria used by the men in our sample as they commented on the ways in which their solicitor was helpful or unhelpful. We were surprised at the amount of richly detailed material many respondents produced in response to our questions. Forty-two of the respondents mentioned both negative and positive aspects of their solicitors' service, twenty-three gave all positive comments, and eleven gave all negative ones. The overall positive balance of comments confirms to some extent the findings from other research. Murch (1980), for example, found that the majority of his sample was satisfied with their solicitor. In the following section we show and discuss the range of comments made but leave the reader to make the final judgment about their usefulness and limitations. Inevitably in attempting to analyse the material some of the richness of the individual case material gets lost. To try to avoid this we have incorporated a number of illustrative comments taken from the questionnaires and interviews.

Comments on Helpfulness

In all there was sixty-two separate comments made about solicitors' helpfulness. These were made up of thirty-nine comments referring to solicitors' legal competence in dealing with the problems presented:

	Number
Demonstrated legal competence	19
Gave helpful advice	10
Gave specific assistance with property settlements, access and financial arrangements and custody	8
Was speedy and efficient	2

Twenty comments made reference to certain personal qualities the solicitor displayed in helping the men through their difficulties:

	Number
Gave me support, understanding and encouragement	7
Showed a helpful manner	7
Demonstrated a willingness to fight on my behalf and protect my rights	6

and three others acknowledged their solicitors as helpful but described the help rather grudgingly. One said, 'he did the work he was supposed to do', another said, 'he did what he was told to do', and the third said, 'only in giving general advice on Legal Aid and the working of the divorce laws'.

The most significant feature of the positive comments is that well over half refer to the solicitors' professional competence and ability in dealing with legal problems—qualities which some might regard as no more than should be expected. Here are some examples:

He was helpful in that he arranged the finances and sorted out the legal side;

He helped me to understand what was going on as the proceedings were taking place and to get the best possible deal out of it;

He processed the whole affair with maximum speed and efficiency;

Full discussion of details in obtaining custody deal and over costs;

He explained the mechanics of divorce—he was prompt in his preparation of a petition and he gave assistance preparing the case for joint custody of the children.

The remainder of the positive comments refer to the solicitors' human relations skills and personal qualities. This is clearly an important dimension. Such skills and qualities include 'being a good listener', 'understanding', 'support with genuine sincerity', 'being friendly' and 'helping to reduce worry'. One man was particularly appreciative of his solicitor's skills and manner:

He took a personal caring approach to his work. Always sympathetic to my case. I always had the impression that to him 'it was not just another case'.

The other important criterion by which solicitors were judged was their willingness to 'fight' for the man or encourage him to 'fight'. Our evidence suggests that the 'partisan' aspect of the solicitor's role is important for some men in giving them confidence and preventing them from 'giving up', 'accepting defeat' and agreeing to imposed settlements. The comments on this aspect of helpfulness reflect how solicitors provided encouragement to contest or fight for more money, or for a better settlement over the property arrangements, or 'not to allow my ex-wife to have her own way'. As one man wrote, 'he managed to get me access; it has taken me two years to have my daughter stay with me and I am very pleased with my solicitor.' Another appreciated the good advice—'to dig my heels in over access and joint ownership of the marital home'. A final comment refers to how 'he protected my interests in all matters'. The high value placed by some on this approach is especially ironic since one of the arguments against the adversarial system is that it encourages 'fighting' and leads to antagonism and unhelpfully long drawn-out battles between the partners, thereby making it difficult to 'end the marriage'. This could reflect, in part, the general expectation that divorce is *expected* to involve a fight and there would be some disappointment if this in fact did not take place. More specifically it could mean that to many men the solicitor is a convenient, and supportive, 'channel' by means of which their feelings of anger and injustice can be directed at the cause of their distress. Whatever the explanation, some men need to feel, and to have demonstrated, that their solicitor is aggressively 'on their side' in sorting matters out. Problems to do with money, property and children involve peoples' rights as well as their needs and wants, and the partisan role is seen to be important in protecting these.

Comments on Unhelpfulness

In all there were seventy-one negative comments made about solicitors, nine more than the number of positive ones. They were:

Gave unhelpful advice	14
Extortionate and high costs	11
Poor communication and briefing (includes difficulties understanding legal jargon and generally unhelpful manner)	11
Very slow and many delays	9
Unwilling to 'fight' on my behalf	8
Demonstrated a low level of professional competence, including making errors and negligence	6
Failed to respond to, and carry out, instructions	4
Provocative and non-conciliatory behaviour which stirred up trouble and caused more problems	4
Lack of awareness about the emotional aspects of divorce	4
	71

It is especially important to note the comments of the six respondents who mention they had female solicitors; four of these report them as unhelpful. One made particular reference to a partisan position: 'my first solicitor was awful and female and I felt she was biased'. The other three stress that their solicitors were female, although their criticisms are about technical incompetence and failure to carry out the client's wishes. The remaining two who employed a female solicitor expressed positive comments. Clearly the numbers are very small and only one man alleges bias. However, it may be that more thought should be given to the possible implications of gender mix when allocating solicitors to their clients. It is quite likely that divorcing men will have strong feelings about women which may influence how they react to a female solicitor no matter how good her advice and intentions. Some of these feelings are hinted at by the man who said, 'I was rather negative towards her instructions and it was the biggest mistake of my life'.

In our sample we also have six men who changed their solicitors once—and a further two who changed their solicitors twice. The reasons given for the changes included:

Staid

A biased female solicitor

Incorrect legal advice about basic rights

Advised that judges do not like men having custody of young children

Nearly lost my home because of an untrained solicitor

Told I would never get joint custody

Outmanoeuvred by my solicitor with the result that I gave full custody and control to my ex-wife without knowing until too late.

It was significant that all those who changed their solicitors expressed positive comments about their eventual one, which in two cases was their third choice. We were therefore left wondering how many others with negative experiences may have benefitted from a change. One of the difficulties of changing is the uncertainty of assessing the alternative standard of service that might be available and what the consequences may be of changing. All we can report is that those who did change indicated it had led to an improvement.

When we looked at the seventy-one negative comments made about solicitors we found that 28 per cent of them referred to legal incompetence or unhelpful advice. Without knowing a lot more details about each of the cases it is difficult to assess how reasonable these comments were. Some referred simply to a lack of information about Legal Aid, basic rights and divorce and legal procedures generally. As one man wrote, 'I learnt more from the *Which* book on Divorce'. Others had much more disturbing comments to make. One wrote, 'I nearly got committed to prison because they did not release my Building Society cash quickly enough to satisfy "her" solicitor'. Another man wrote, 'Only advice, to change my name and leave the country . . . worse than useless', and another complained that 'he gave very little advice, just agreeing to write to my wife's solicitor with whatever I wished to say or do but with very little guidance'. Others are clear in their assessment of his ignorance of the law. As one man wrote, 'he did not know too much about the law' and another, 'not much knowledge of family law. Bad advice'. Even more disturbing are two instances where the complaint refers to negligence by the solicitor in 'failing to answer the petition and prepare the case on two occasions over custody of the children' and in the other to the solicitor's 'refusal to listen to medical evidence, which showed the health of my ex-wife was deteriorating'. Whatever the accuracy of these criticisms they do show how negatively a fair number of men assessed the legal advice given and the competence shown.

The next two largest categories of comment are those which relate to high costs and poor communications and briefing. All the references to high costs include other negative comments which seem to suggest that costs in themselves are not the crucial factor in assessing helpfulness but that they become significant when other factors are deemed unhelpful. Here are several examples:

Vague about possible interpretation of the law. Frequently made errors of judgment. Very expensive.

I went to them for advice and found out that due to my ignorance I was used to get their bill up as high as they could get it . . . £900 paid nine years later!

A lot of letters for which I was being charged to inflate the costs on both sides.

He lost me my children, my home, all my capital and a massive maintenance settlement and cost a great deal of money.

He tried to stir up complications and introduce unnecessary delays, presumably to increase the overall cost.

Taken too long so they can get more costs from me.

Two others, who had overall positive experiences, simply comment, 'expensive' and 'very costly' regarding the unhelpful aspects of their solicitors. Although most of the comments cited about legal charges contain little hard information, they do indicate that costs are an important criterion for many men in assessing their solicitors' performance. It is also noticeable that several men saw it as helpful that their solicitor explained how the costs were arrived at and allowed them time to pay. As one man (a doctor) wrote, 'He allowed me to pay off his fees over 25 years'.

Amongst the eleven men who referred to poor communication and briefing, there were two who refer to the difficulties of understanding legal language. As one said, 'he spoke in legal language which I did not grasp half the time'. Other criticisms in this category relate to a generally unhelpful manner in carrying out the work.

Here are some examples:

She failed to carry out my wishes to defend the petition. Difficult to contact. Did not explain divorce procedures to me. Worried me about financial aspects.

He did not co-operate or follow my instructions.

He refused to clear up ambiguous court order created partly by his negligence, her solicitor, and partly by the court. [this related to defining access].

He had a short-sighted attitude.

Always being in a rush when I saw him.

Seemed very indifferent to my problems.

Given that amongst the positive comments on helpfulness many referred to the important human qualities shown by the solicitor, it is perhaps not surprising that when these are absent a negative assessment is made.

Closely related to this category are the eight comments which refer to solicitors' negative attitudes towards contesting or 'fighting' the cases. One man wrote: 'I felt he was more interested in my ex-wife's side of things. Eventually I did the divorce myself without legal help'. Other comments under this heading include: 'Very negative attitude, defeatist attitude'; 'He did not attempt to "win" the most "favourable" terms'. Several men refer to the negative attitude shown by their solicitors when giving advice about important issues to do with children and finances:

Negative attitude regarding my chance of getting custody of my daughter which I now understand were good at the time my wife left.

They said judges do not like men having custody of young children. [He subsequently changed his solicitor.]

He advised no chance concerning custody, care and control and maintenance.

When I asked for joint custody I was told 'you'll never get it'. [He subsequently changed his solicitor.]

One man, who 'lost' his children and 'lost' his property complained about his solicitor's advice to 'surrender' rather than to 'fight' either of these issues. It is clear that this man felt that he had been 'let down', which is a phrase used by another man who contested and lost a custody case. In the same way that several men expressed positive comments about how they valued their solicitors' willingness to 'fight' on their behalf or encourage them to, it is perhaps not surprising, when this initiative is lacking, that some men will judge their solicitors as unhelpful. It should be restated that we are not presuming to judge whether the advice given by solicitors was legally appropriate or accurate. We are concerned to show how this advice was perceived and evaluated by their clients. It is clear that the manner, attitudes and qualities of solicitors are important criteria by which men judge their services, and that when these are judged negatively it is more likely that the help, advice and overall service will not be valued.

Amongst the remaining categories the important comments refer to the specifically provocative and non-conciliatory behaviour of some solicitors, their slowness and delays in conducting affairs, and a general lack of awareness of the emotional aspects of divorcing. In all, these constituted 24 per cent of the negative comments made. The following illustrates the ways in which men found their solicitors to be provocative and non-conciliatory:

He tried to stir up complications.

He tended to state things in a way which I knew would provoke adverse reactions.

Although my ex-wife and self approached him jointly for advice on maintenance, etc., he appeared to assume *conflict* and as a result gave mistaken advice which cost us quite a lot jointly.

Not really attuned to conciliation matters regarding access.

Some other men commented in more general terms about the impossible position of the solicitor in acting as a conciliator or negotiator. The most articulate was the man who said:

His role is a nonsense negotiating any agreement. For all that, I felt some sympathy with him as a person. It was evident that the protracted divorce procedures actually required a mediator and not an advocate. The current structure seems absurd except as a last resort!

Another more extravagant comment was:

'With the best will in the world there is little he can do to stop you getting "screwed".'

Those who referred to delays and the length of time taken included some who felt very negative about their solicitor and some who on balance judged him as helpful. Some assumed delays were related to increasing costs, whilst others were simply irritated with the amount of time taken. The irritation is reflected in the brusqueness of the comments:

He took an extremely long time to do it;
Very slow;

He dragged out all the proceedings.

Adversary, Counsellor or Mediator?

The critical comments concerning the solicitor's lack of awareness of emotional aspects and his or her provocative and non-conciliatory approach to issues raise an important question. To what extent *should* a solicitor be expected to provide moral support as well as legal guidance? One man thought that perhaps it was 'probably quite right' that solicitors were not able to deal with the emotional aspects even though he used this inability as a criticism of his solicitor. In Murch's study, '. . . they were frequently ascribed a counselling role. In this respect they were surprisingly viewed more favourably than most other professional workers' (apart from doctors and divorce court welfare officers). Murch's view is that this may be due to the solicitor being a more acceptable form of social support and the fact that 'the solicitor's counselling role was often performed implicitly'.

To what extent, too, should the solicitor act automatically in a heavily partisan way regardless, perhaps, of his or her private views and with closer regarded to winning a conflict rather than negotiating a balanced settlement? We looked at the range of comments which bore on this question. Six positive comments refer to the helpful value placed on the solicitor's 'fighting spirit' or his ability to stimulate his clients to 'fight'. Eight negative comments refer to the unhelpfulness of their solicitor when there is an absence of either of these skills. A further eight comments refer to the un-helpfulness of their solicitor *because* of his 'provocative' and 'non-conciliatory' behaviour and lack of awareness of the emotional aspects of divorce.

The numbers in the three groups are too small to draw firm con-clusions and we would not want them to be used as evidence for one school of thought or another. We are aware however that the issues of fighting, conciliation and lack of emotional awareness of solicitors are important for a number of our respondents. Out of the total of 133 helpful and unhelpful comments they are mentioned twenty-two times (17 per cent). From comments made during our interviews several men expected their solicitors to be on 'their' side and 'put up a good show'. The fear of losing property, children and money generates strong emotions. One man, for example, bitterly regretted he had not instructed his solicitor to take a 'firmer line earlier'. Another was in danger of accepting a less than 50 per cent settlement on the original matrimonial home, which he had build and financed, and was wondering whether he should challenge the offer in the courts! It is perhaps not surprising that 'fighting' remains an important part of the solicitor's expected role when such decisions have to be made. Solicitors are presented with a dilemma of how to protect their clients' legal rights and promote their best interests without at the same time provoking emotional conflict and upset between the parties. Clearly some of our sample feel that where the solicitor's allegiance is weak, which is reflected in his reluctance to 'fight', he is of little help.

In the present debate about the adversarial role and the place of the courts in all divorce matters, it may be useful to differentiate between the two main issues involved in post-divorce settlements (property and children) and see whether each one requires a different approach, based on a different principle. Decisions over property, assets and money, etc. have a very substantial effect on a man's ability to build a new life. Such decisions are about justice and fairness, which is where solicitors and the courts have an important part to play. Moreover, since the outcomes will affect both parties ultimately it may be somewhat naive to assume that agreeable settlements can be reached by negotiation and consent, however hard the parties and their advisers might try. Money generates strong emotions, which should not be used as the basis for making decisions. Berry's suggestion that there should be a family tribunal, chaired by a 'numerate administrator for determining financial issues, including division of assets' (*The Times*, 7 January 1981) implies that the decisions would be accepted as fair and just by both parties. This view perhaps reflects an overreliance on rationality and an assumption that it is solely the legal process—the courts and solicitors—which generates the emotional energy. No doubt current court procedures and the adversarial system generally often *exacerbate* strong emotions, but this is not the same as arguing that they cause them. Our evidence has already shown that many men feel extremely angry about the legal process they experienced. From our interviews with some of them it is difficult to see how an alternative system of adjudicating over important financial and property matters would lessen these feelings and lead to more acceptable settlements. More thought needs to be given to helping men deal with the angry and bitter feelings, and the various conciliation services attached to courts would seem to be a valuable way forward. But in the end it does seem from our evidence concerning financial and property settlements, that in a number of cases there may be no way of bypassing strongly-felt feelings which linger on following the break-up.

With regard to settlements over children, however, the issues are very different. The essential differences are that children also have rights, needs and feelings with regard to their own welfare and their relationships with both their parents, and that the relationships continue after the settlements. Disputes, protracted court hearings, and an atmosphere which tends to exacerbate fighting feelings, are not the best contexts for these complex decisions to be made, or for setting the most appropriate tone for future relationships. The 1966 Law Commission Report (English Law Commission, 1966) recognised that the objective of a good divorce law in relation to children would be to 'encourage harmonious relationships between the parties and their children in the future'. Berry argues that from his experience of working with Families Need Fathers this aim has never been achieved because 'lawyers are simply not the right people for the job'. He argues that the 'losers' are 'the children when parent is set against parent'.

There are two distinct issues involved in the present debate. One is how best to protect and safeguard the children's rights and promote their welfare, and the other concerns the rights of fathers with regard to their children. Finding a satisfactory system which balances both justice for the father and mother with the welfare of the child is extremely difficult, as has been evidenced in the debate over how best to deal with juvenile offenders. Welfare and justice do not rest easily together. There may well be instances where from the welfare point of view the child's interests may best be promoted by preventing one of the parents having contact. From a judicial point of view this may be deemed unjust. Only in an ideal world could all the parties involved arrive at a just and mutually beneficial arrangement. From our evidence some parents manage to find a modus vivendi for balancing these issues, but there are others, perhaps a larger number, where the injustice of the decisions continues to rankle and the future welfare of all those involved is clearly prejudiced.

Alternative Proposals

One alternative basis for promoting children's welfare would involve two different forms of marriage contract, one for childless couples and one for those with children. In the former case the present contract would be sufficient but in the latter case couples would be expected to make a more binding contractual commitment of at least ten or fifteen years to stay together whilst the children are in their formative years and when their social and emotional needs are greatest. Such a contract would be much more difficult to terminate than at present. This is much more in line with Polish Family Law which forbids divorce by couples with children unless the court is fully satisfied with the detailed arrangements for the continued parenting of the children. The counter argument is that it would be a retrograde step and probably be counter-productive as couples would find other means of 'divorcing' and 'separating' outside the law. We discuss a proposal of this sort at the end of the book.

A less radical solution proposed by the All Party Divorce Law Reform Group would be to tighten the court's application of the present law with regard to children's welfare. They have argued that no decree absolute should be granted until the court accepts that the arrangements for the children that have been made 'are satisfactory or the best that can be arranged in the circumstances' (Clause 41 of the Matrimonial Causes Act 1973) and are in keeping with the overall child's welfare needs. But who is to act as adviser to the courts and how realistic is it in terms of time and available resources for all cases involved to be investigated?

At present only one in ten cases is referred to the court welfare officer for investigation. The All Party Group believes that the number of disputes over children would be lessened if custody was normally awarded to both parents; such a change would encourage more serious attention being given to the welfare needs of the children by the divorcing couple and the solicitors, since they would no longer be fighting over custody.

An alternative system for resolving divorce cases was put forward by the Finer Committee (1974) which advocated the establishment of a Family Court for dealing with all legal matters affecting family life. They saw this court operating more on a fact-finding basis than the present adversarial one. Many divorce lawyers support this view. Moreover the Committee saw the importance of providing a conciliation service attached to the courts. By conciliation they meant:

Assisting the parties to deal with the consequences of the established breakdown of their marriage, whether resulting in a divorce or in a separation, by reaching agreements or giving consents or reducing the area of conflict upon custody, support, access to and education of the children, financial provision, the disposition of the matrimonial home, lawyers' fees and every other matter arising from the breakdown which calls for decision on future matters.

The Working Party on Marriage Guidance (1979) strongly supported the Finer propositions, particularly that relating to a court-based conciliation service. In their analysis they argue that the Finer Committee is distinguishing between the judicial and welfare issues following divorce. Whereas the function of the courts is judicial, the main purpose of the conciliation service would be 'to help individuals and couples to sort out their views, attitudes and feelings—make decisions which are most beneficial to the mental and emotional health of themselves, their spouses, and their children, and begin to adapt themselves to the implications of these decisions.

Neither the Finer proposals nor those of the Working Party have been implemented. However groups of solicitors, social workers, probation officers and other supporters of family courts, have started to set up their own informal conciliation services. A pioneer scheme was established in Bristol in 1979 under the title of the Bristol Family Courts Conciliation Service. The co-ordinator of the scheme believes that it provides 'an opportunity in a neutral, informal and non-judgemental setting for separating and divorcing couples to explore the possibilities of reaching agreements over matters that would otherwise, in all probability, be contested in court.' The early evidence is that in a substantial proportion of cases where both parties were involved, agreement was reached on the issue which had been referred by the court. This scheme and others, which are being set up, look to have much merit for all the couples who want to reach agreements. However, the problem that remains is how to help those who are *not* willing to seek settlements out of court, or even at all, or those where only one party wants a resolution by these means.

Fathers' Rights

In Chapter 7 we discuss some of the difficulties fathers have with custody and access arrangements and in maintaining contact with their children when the mother has the day-to-day care and control of the children. Many of the difficulties in the period following a court decision stem from the advice given and attitudes shown by some solicitors towards fathers who either seek sole or even joint custody and fathers who want frequent access to their children. If the advice is discouraging it is likely that either the petition will be dropped by the father or, if it goes to court, it will not be presented as strongly as the father would wish. To add to these problems, courts have a general reluctance to grant sole custody to fathers unless there are exceptional circumstances. In our survey only eight fathers were granted sole custody and in each case the wife did not contest the petition. In three other cases there were split custody arrangements. In the eight sole custody cases the mother had left the children with their father at the time of the break-up and in four of these cases the mother had serious mental health problems so in all these cases the issue really determined itself. There were a further eighteen fathers who unsuccessfully contested the custody and four who wanted to contest custody but were either advised against such an action by their solicitor or were effectively kept in ignorance of their right to do so.

The general advice offered by one commentator to fathers who want custody of their children summarises the problem, '. . . keep the children from the point of separation away from the wife. He does not have as good a chance as the mother, and he may have to rely on some particular defect on her part, but his maintenance of the status quo is the only real way he can hope for justice from the judges at present. All litigation is a risk and sometimes he may lose' (article in *The Times*, 9 March 1980). Such advice might be alright for the small minority of fathers where the mother leaves the children but offers little comfort to the great majority of fathers who themselves move out of the matrimonial home after the break-up. The major criticism voiced by many fathers of the existing practice is the denial and non-acceptance by both solicitors and courts that fathers also have rights in relation to their children and that divorce from the mother does not mean that they have abdicated their duties and responsibilities towards the children. Many fathers recognise the real and practical difficulties of having the day-to-day care and control of their children, particularly those of pre-school age but they are concerned to play a continuing role in their children's lives after divorce. The consequence of the continuing failure of the courts actively to value and recognise the role of fathers can contribute to the subsequent difficulties over access and maintaining contact with their children. The advice of the solicitor and the manner in which it is given can influence many fathers' feelings, attitudes and behaviour towards their ex-wives which in turn affects the quality and extent of contact with their children. All these difficulties were summed up by one man who said, 'I divorced my wife; I did not divorce my children.'

Conclusion

There are many improvements that could be made to the machinery of the law, including the drawing up of a register of competent divorce solicitors; a monitoring of the services with particular attention given to clients' views; guidelines for solicitors' practice; better availability of counselling services to be called in by solicitors when the problems go beyond their expertise and understanding and much better co-ordination of the services available to help divorced men with their many problems. Improvements in each of these areas would lead to a more effective and sensitive legal system for dealing with post-divorce problems without giving undue weight to non-judicial welfare or counselling services in deciding issues which affect peoples' legal rights and freedoms. There is a clear need for court-based counselling/conciliation services but their role will continue to be limited by the willingness of both parties to agree to negotiate and mutually accept the outcomes. It is doubtful whether *any* new system will be able to cope with all the problems. The emotions generated by breaking up are considerable. As the Working Party (1979) point out, 'the divorce process is (thus) often accompanied by feelings of uncertainty, sadness, panic, bitterness or regret, or even reluctance.' These common human reactions will not altogether disappear as a result of changing the legal system for a more welfare-based conciliation scheme.

Chapter 7
The Subsequent Effects

Reaction to Loss and Change

Individual reactions to the stresses of divorce range across a continuum from those who negotiate the breakdown of their marriage without acrimony and who go on to make a new life whilst maintaining a good relationship with their ex-spouse to those who are both unable to accept the reality of the divorce and who fail to set about making a new start. Each individual's response across the continuum is unique but there are common threads to the experience. For the majority divorce is a trauma which takes years to come to terms with.

The experience of divorce often contains the major elements of a bereavement—a total upheaval of the pattern of life; an inability to accept the reality of what has happened; a searching for the lost partner; anger and outbursts of rage; despair, an overwhelming sense of loss. Divorce lacks the finality of death. It is common for divorcees to express the view that it would be so much easier if the ex-partner were actually dead. In divorce it is the marriage that dies; the partner is very much alive and often seemingly larger than life. It is possible; especially for those who oppose the divorce, to hold on to the hope of re-establishing the marriage and thus avoid the painful reality that confronts them. The denial and disbelief can be channelled into fantasies of reunion or of a new start long after the marriage has ended. The degree of trauma experienced is in part influenced by the nature of the marriage. A partner who has been cold and rejecting for many years may not be missed as much as one who despite difficulties has been a close ally or confidante. However, even where the marriage has been very unhappy and a partner abusive or cruel the act of divorce signals a failure which is painfully felt and is often perceived as humiliation.

In contrast to bereavement where feelings of anger and hostility against the lost person are not generally socially acceptable, in divorce they are not only felt but are often openly expressed. The disappointment at the failure of the marriage may act as the catalyst that extinguishes the last traces of good feelings in a marriage. The anger and rage is expressed through prolonged battles over property, money, and child care. For a small but significant group, often those bitterly opposed to the divorce, the anger and hostility reach a pitch akin to hatred. For this group their energy is tied up in vindictive and abusive thoughts and actions. This group has been labelled by Wallerstein and Kelly (1980) as 'embittered and chaotic'. The desire to hit back, to score points off the ex-partner becomes the organising principle behind much of their life.

The way in which individuals differ in their reaction to loss is not only influenced by the qualities of the marriage or the circumstances of its break-up but also by the individual's personality. Marriage is an important source of self-esteem. It confers social status and confirms belief in self-worth and meaning. The break-up is often felt as personal failure and evidence of an inability to love or care or simply to be successful. Individuals with low self-esteem prior to divorce who already have a negative view of themselves and their abilities are prone to interpret the breakdown as further evidence of personal failings. They are also more likely to interpret it as their fault and feel guilt ridden as a consequence. The experience of previous losses such as bereavement as a child or a broken home may strongly colour an individual's reaction. The breaking of the bond with the spouse may reawaken previous conflicts and hurt.

In marriages with children the response is further complicated for the spouse who ceases to live with the children by the loss not only of the spouse but also of the family unit. As will be demonstrated later, this additional loss sometimes has a profound effect and greatly increases the degree of trauma experienced. A sense of despair and hopelessness, a loss of interest in work, friendships and unpredictable mood swings are felt by many. In a significant proportion of cases these feelings reach a level where they actually become clinically depressed. They suffer sleep disturbance, loss of appetite, have suicidal ideas, and may make suicidal attempts, both successful and unsuccessful. They suffer severe problems of concentration and withdraw from other people.

Wallerstein and Kelly in their study of sixty divorcing couples found that at five years after separation over half the adults in their study were functioning well psychologically. However, one-third of the men and one-fifth of the women were still moderately troubled and continued to be depressed, suicidal, alcoholic or had substantial difficulties in relating to other adults. On the other hand, as with other personal crises, the process of coming to terms with what has happened and rebuilding afresh after divorce offers opportunities for personal growth and maturation. With acceptance of the separation many come to see the break-up as having been beneficial and report feeling they have an improved quality of life. In this chapter and the next we discuss some of the positive, as well as the negative, changes experienced by the ninety-two men in our study.

Effects on Health

The process of divorce and separation can have profound effects on both physical and mental health. There is a large body of evidence which suggests that the stresses associated with divorce exact a high price in terms of illness. The relationship between divorce and ill health is not a simple one, as health problems can contribute to marital breakdown as well as marital breakdown, for some, precipitating ill health. A study in the early 1970s by the American National Centre for Health Statistics looked at differential health characteristics as a function of marital status in a total of 88,000 households. These results showed markedly raised rates of illness and disability over a number of measures of health. They found, for example, that divorced men had on average 25.6 days per year of restricted activity due to health problems as against married men who had 16.2 days of restricted activity.

In our study the subjects were asked to give details of physical illness since the time of their divorce and, if they had been ill, whether they had suffered the illness before they were divorced. The results were as follows:

	Number	Percentage
New physical health problems	26	28
Pre-existing physical health problems	6	7
Total with physical health problems	32	35
No physical health problems	60	65
	92	100

Of the twenty-six reporting new physical health problems, eleven detailed illness es that are frequently associated with severe stress, such as stomach ulcers, skin conditions, chest pains and migraine attacks. Without a matched sample of non-divorced men little can be directly concluded from the high incidence of illness in our sample. It is however, in line with the growing body of evidence which links stress to increased disease morbidity.

Prominent amongst the work in this area is that of Holmes and Rahe (1967) who developed a scale of stressful life events which has shown both prospectively and retrospectively that people experiencing high levels of stress are more likely to become ill. Their scale for measuring the impact of life events was derived by asking 400 subjects to compare different life events and getting them to attribute scores to events according to the degree of life change they thought they involved. The scale they derived by this means scores divorce as second only to death of spouse as a lifechange event. It ranks higher than detention in jail, being fired from work, retirement, pregnancy and death of a close friend. The greater the life change scores the greater is the likelihood of health problems. In addition to the raised incidence of disease, divorced individuals also show an increased vulnerability to accidents. McMurray (1970) demonstrated that the motor vehicle accident rate of persons undergoing divorce doubled during the six months before and six months after the divorce date.

The impact of divorce on mental health is much more marked for men than for women. Admission rates to psychiatric hospitals are lowest for married people and highest for the divorced and separated. A study by Grad and Sainsbury (1966) revealed raised psychiatric referral rates for the divorced and separated and a ratio of these rates to the rates of married persons of the order 10:1 for men and 4:1 for females. As with physical illness, caution is needed in interpreting such studies as mental health problems themselves can lead to marital breakdown.

In our own study, the strong association that exists between divorce and mental health problems was supported. The men were asked if they had been mentally ill or had mental health problems since their divorce and whether they had suffered with these problems prior to divorce. They were also asked whether they had taken anti-depressants or tranquillisers and sleeping tablets before, during or after the divorce. Their responses were used to assign them to one of the categories listed below. Those categorised as having suffered very severe mental health problems reported, for example, difficulties of such severity that they were hospitalised or were unable to work for a considerable period. Those categorised as having suffered minor mental health problems reported for example transitory difficulties in sleeping or short periods of anxiety.

The number of men assigned to each category was as follows:

	Number	Percentage
New very severe mental health problems	8	9
New severe mental health problems	22	24
New mental health problems	24	26
New very minor mental health problems	8	9
Total of new mental health problems	62	68
Pre-existing very severe mental health problems	0	0
Pre-existing severe mental health problems	4	4
Pre-existing mental health problems	5	5
Pre-existing very minor mental health problems	1	1
No mental health problems	20	22
	92	100

The use of medication was as follows:

	Number	Percentage
Anti-depressants and/or tranquillisers:		
Before divorce	12	13
Over period of divorce	29	33
After divorce	23	25
At time of survey	13	14
Sleeping pills:		
Before divorce	6	7
Over period of divorce	14	15
After divorce	13	14
At time of survey	12	13

As can be seen from these results, approximately one-third of the men in our sample suffered from very severe or severe mental health problems and only 4 per cent of these reported their difficulties pre-dating their divorce. A third also had recourse to anti-depressant and/or tranquillising medication and 15 per cent took sleeping tablets. The most commonly reported problem was depression which was mentioned by 30 per cent of the sample.

The men in the study were also asked whether they had experienced a number of specific symptoms and if so whether they had also experienced them prior to their divorce. The percentages of men who experienced the particular symptoms are shown below.

Symptom	Percentage	Experienced prior to divorce (percentages)
Sleep problems	53	18
Increased irritability	50	12
Excessive worrying	49	19
Strong changes of mood	44	18
Loss of appetite	27	2
Loss of sexual interest	27	9
Headaches	25	12

These results are compatible with the high incidence of depression reported. As can be seen around half suffered with some sleep disturbance, and/or excessive worry and/or increased irritability and over a quarter experienced some loss of sexual interest. Only three men reported attempting suicide. Studies have shown a high rate of suicide for divorced individuals, and in many countries the rate is approximately double that of married persons.

The high percentage of men experiencing new mental health problems in our sample illustrates the degree of personal trauma that divorce involves. Why the psychiatric casualty rate after divorce is higher for men than for women can only be speculated about. One argument is that men gain more from marriage than women and are in consequence harder hit when it collapses. Also of importance may be men's socialisation that encourages the inhibition of emotional expression and thereby the 'working through' of the pain and unhappiness. Another contributory factor is likely to be the multiple loss for men. Very often it is not only the loss of a wife and at least a partial loss of the fathering role but also career damage and reduction in standard of living.

A not untypical account of the months after the break-up of a marriage was given by one of our sample. He had been married fifteen years and had a boy of 11 and a girl of 12 when his wife left to live with another man, taking the children with her. He had never before experienced any mental health problems. From the moment of her departure right through the period of their divorce he was seriously depressed. In his own words, 'I was completely and utterly shattered.' For the six months after her departure, he had great difficulty in getting off to sleep and when asleep was wakened by nightmares and dreams involving his wife. He was spending much of his time alone in tears and tormented by thoughts of his wife with the other man. He was able to keep working but lost all interest in it and at his own request was demoted to a job of less responsibility. His sleep problems did not abate and his smoking increased to between sixty and seventy cigarettes a day. He was put on anti-depressant medication by his doctor three months after the break-up. His depressed mood, his negative view of himself and his despondency about the future lifted slowly and only after the divorce was concluded a year later did his mental state return to normal. Three years after his divorce he was again enjoying his work and had a fairly active social life and felt himself to have 'gotten over' the break-up. Looking back on his emotional response to it he summed up his experience: 'If there is hell on earth, I've been there.'

Effects on the Role as a Father

VISITING FATHERS

Divorce involves major changes in the behaviour of all those involved. Reconstructing relationships, rebuilding self-esteem, unlearning and relearning ways of relating to children when one parent is absent and generally coming to terms with failure and all that has taken place in the marriage are some of the unavoidable tasks which face divorcing couples. For some the break-up comes as a welcome relief and allows for a fresh start whilst for others it is incomprehensible and damaging and leaves scars of bitterness and anger for years to come. Learning to adapt and readapt one's life is complex and difficult enough but it is made worse by the absence of any socially agreed pattern of social behaviour for divorced people. Nowhere is this deficiency seen more clearly than in the position of a father who has not been granted custody of his children, in other words a 'visiting' or 'part-time father'. On the one hand the law expects him to continue economic provision for his children, and on the other he is expected to behave 'reasonably' and 'fairly' over his rights to access and contact with his children. If he is too demanding he can be considered unfair and unrealistic but if he has too little or no contact he can be seen as irresponsible and indifferent to his children. There is little formal assistance available to help him learn what his new role entails and how he might exercise it in the best interests of the children. If either he or his ex-wife remarries or has a new partner the problems are increased and the ambiguity of the new role is accentuated.

This lack of agreement about the 'visiting' or 'part-time' father's role is highlighted in a recent study by Wallerstein and Kelly (1980);

> the relationship between the visiting parent and the visited child of course has no counterpart and therefore no model within the intact family. Its parameters, its limits, and its potentialities are new and remain to be explored . . . the parent who moves out of the household begins a new role for which there is no dress rehearsal and no script.

What is the new role? Is it that of friend, guest, or parent? What are the rules, expectations and limits which underpin it? In short, how should visiting fathers behave?

Coping with the loss of a partner and in many instances the loss of the children as well clearly has deep-seated effects on men's views of themselves. Father and husband are accepted terms for describing status in our society. When either one of these collapses the repercussions on one's identity can be considerable and the task of rebuilding a new self-image can be slow and lengthy. The loss can be likened to that of losing a limb. In this section we are principally concerned with examining the ways in which fathers adapted to, and learnt from, the loss of the active father role following the break-up of the original family unit.

Frequency of contact. We decided to study these adaptations partly by examining the frequency of contact between 'visiting fathers' and their children. In all there are sixty-six such fathers with at least one child under the age of sixteen. In the questionnaire we asked them to state how many times in the past month they had had contact with their children. A small number indicated the irrelevance of this time boundary and gave details of their contact over an average year. This material has been recalculated and combined with the majority who gave a monthly answer. It needs to be emphasised that we are not discussing the *quality* of the contact or its effects on the parents involved. This would have necessitated an analysis of the children's and the fathers' experiences. However the quantitative material is important in that if fathers have had little or no contact in the past month this in itself tells us something of the quality of the relationship. We focus first on the cases in which either the mother was granted sole custody or where there was a joint custody order, but care and control was with the mother. The group of eight fathers granted sole custody, plus another three where there were split custody decisions, was too small to analyse in a similar way. The special features of these cases are discussed later.

Fifty-six non-custodial fathers responded to the question about how many times in the past month they had had contact with their children. The results are as follows:

	Number of contacts in past month									
	0	1	2	3	4	6	7	10	16	Not yet finalised
Number of fathers (56 in all)	26*	8	6	2	8	2	1	1	1	1

Note: * This includes a split custody arrangement and is not included in the analysis of fathers with nil contact

We thus see that nearly half of these fathers had not had any contact with their children in the past month. A further quarter (14) had contact with their children only once or twice, ten had contact three or four times, and only six more than four times. From the children's point of view this means that nearly three-quarters had had little or no contact with their father in the past month. It seems clear that most fathers would like to have *more* contact with their children: thirty-eight (70 per cent) of the fifty-four fathers who replied to this question on our questionnaire would like to see more of their children and only sixteen (30 per cent) are satisfied with the contact arrangements.

Distance and Remarriage. In view of the large proportion of fathers who would like to have more contact, we examined whether the distance between the father and the children, and whether or not he had remarried, helped to explain the amount of contact. Amongst the twenty-five no-contact fathers distance alone did not appear to be the main factor, as eleven (44 per cent) lived less than twenty miles away from the children. However, amongst the thirty fathers in contact with their children, twenty-one (70 per cent) lived within twenty miles. It appears as if proximity may increase contact if other conditions are right but it by no means ensures contact. A similar picture emerges when one looks at the differences between the two groups in terms of whether they are remarried or not. Amongst the no-contact fathers, those that are remarried tend to live a lot further away than those who are not remarried. This might help to explain why the non-remarried group of fathers seems to be in closer contact with their children than those who have remarried; 65 per cent of the non-remarried fathers had seen their children three or more times in the past month compared with only 20 per cent of those who had remarried.

The evidence from Wallerstein and Kelly's work on children's reactions to absent fathers suggests that many children yearn for them rather than avoid them and it therefore appears unlikely that the nil-contact and the low frequency cases can be explained simply by the children's wish not to see their fathers. It was also clear that the majority of both the no-contact and contact fathers would like to see more of their children, which suggests that the reasons are not related to the father's lack of motivation. Although the numbers are too small to draw firm conclusions the picture to emerge is that those who have not remarried and who live close to their children are likely to have a good deal of contact. It also seems that the further away remarried fathers live, the less contact they are likely to have with their children. It is noticeable that fathers who have not remarried tend to live closer to their children than those who have. However we are left with a surprisingly high number of fathers who live nearby but are not in contact with their children. These require some special consideration.

Fathers not in Contact. In the eight no-contact cases where the father is *remarried* the special difficulties are set out overleaf. In response to our question concerning the ways their relationship with their children has been affected by the separation, *each of these eight in different ways described how he was unable to play the expected father role.* Some saw themselves as being more like an

	Number of times mentioned
Obstruction by ex-wife	4
Second wife of father objects	1
Court stopped access	1
Children's resentment of father's new partner	1
Child disturbed by access	1
Distance (in all three cases the children live overseas)	3
	11

uncle, others felt that their children no longer saw them as fathers, others again referred to the difficulties of expressing physical affection and love to their children, and exercising influence over them at school or in their leisure pursuits.

It is interesting that all these eight fathers were able to say something of the changes in their relationship even though they have had no contact with their children in the previous month. Their responses suggest that they are describing what their relationship was like when they last had contact or when they lived together—and that they are using their memories as the basis for their current assessment of the relationship. It also shows how some fathers have adapted to the loss of contact by tending to lay the blame for the changes and the non-contact on either the ex-partner or the children's response to their changed status, rather than themselves accepting some responsibility for confronting the losses and inventing new ways of managing the changed circumstances and overcoming the obstacles

One father whom we interviewed highlights some of the difficulties. His two children are 17 and 15 and until a few months previously he had seen them quite frequently since the divorce eight years ago. He described the relationship as 'reasonable, given the circumstances'. The contact has now broken down because his second wife resents the financial burden imposed on them by his ex-wife and particularly by his elder son who is staying on at school to take 'O' and 'A' levels—'She feels she works to keep my ex-wife and children'. This resentment has placed strains on the second marriage and the man's work. He is faced with the dilemma of saving his new marriage or keeping contact with his children; he has decided to choose the former and is now seeking help. This man sees the difficulties as primarily 'caused' by his ex-wife and his children's resentful attitude towards both him and his present wife. These resentments have in turn triggered off resentment by his second wife.

When one looks at the access difficulties mentioned by those fathers with no contact, but who are *not* remarried, a similar picture emerges:

	Number of times mentioned
Obstruction by ex-wife and/or her family	7
Access seriously affected by distance	3
Stopped by a Court Ruling	2
Doctor's advice regarding father's health	1
Probation Officer's advice	1
Father's decision not to have contact	1
Other, including school holidays, cost, lack of adequate accommodation, 'nowhere to go'.	7
	22

Obstruction by the former wife and in some instances by her family are the commonest problems cited in both the remarried and non-remarried groups of fathers who have no contact. It is noticeable how, apart from one father who decided not to have any more contact, all the fathers perceive the difficulties in terms of the obstructive attitudes and behaviour of others. There is no evidence that fathers in this group have been able to devise a strategy to change or renegotiate the relationships with their children and their ex-wife. Some of those who have had contact in the past have given up the struggle as they have received little or no confirmation of their role as a father. This is highlighted by one father who was actually challenged by his former wife to justify why he wanted to see his children. Perhaps it is not surprising that faced with such a challenge the father eventually gave up and stopped seeing them.

The difficulties of managing the new father role and the strangeness of no longer being influential and valued are even more strongly expressed by most of the non-remarried fathers when they describe the changes in their relationships with their children. Three explicitly explain their no-contact in terms of their experience of no longer seeing themselves as a father figure. Their justification is reinforced by perceiving their children as not wanting to know them. It is as if the behaviour associated with the new role needs validation and confirmation from either the ex-wife or the children. If neither responds positively, and the fathers' self-esteem is low or fragile, they give up trying to keep in touch or rebuild their relationships. The negative changes they feel in their relationships with their children are summarised as follows:

	Number of times mentioned
No longer feel like a 'proper father'	8
Can't keep in touch with their lives, interests, etc.	6
Relationship non-existent	4
Children's negative attitude towards father	2
Complete breakdown of relationship	2
Children's emotional difficulties	2
	24

The group of fathers who have had *no* contact with their children in the previous month is made up mostly of fathers who have tried to maintain contact with their children but have given up because they experience the external barriers as insurmountable. There are only two who, in their comments, accept some of the responsibility for the breakdown in the relationship with their children. On this evidence it appears that non-contact results from obstructive attitudes and behaviour by the ex-wife and a lack of confirmation of the new role by their children. Wallerstein and Kelly (1980) describe the new relationship between visiting fathers and their children as 'fragile' and even under the best circumstances fathers need encouragement and support if the relationship is to develop. Where these are lacking or insufficient the father is likely to see less of his children. This, in turn, is likely to lead to a lowering of expectations by the children and a subsequent diminution in the self-esteem and sense of self-identity of the father. In other words the process may well be self-reinforcing.

Adapting to the new role of visiting father, and constructing a new relationship as a part-time parent, is a complex and time consuming activity. The process would be difficult enough if that was the only task facing visiting fathers, but they also have to cope with all the feelings related to the break-up of their marriage as well as the economic and legal problems which need to be settled after divorce. In short fathers have to rediscover their new identity as men as well as to learn their new role as visiting father. It would seem that amongst our no-contact fathers the external barriers have proved either insurmountable or the struggle to overcome them has proved too costly. We now look at the characteristics of those fathers who *have* had contact with the their children in the previous month to see what factors differentiate the two groups.

Fathers in contact. When one looks at the contact fathers' perceptions of the changes in their relationship with their children, the comments are quite similar to those made by the no-contact fathers. There are sixteen different negative comments, with the majority referring to changes in the children's behaviour towards them. Phrases like 'wary', 'cautious', 'distant', 'careful' and don't want to offend' are commonly cited. Other fathers describe the changes in terms of them feeling 'out of touch', 'distant', 'partial strangers' and 'no depth' in relationship with their children. However, when one looks at the eleven positive changes cited, there is an important insight into the differences between the contact and no-contact fathers. Many of those in contact refer to their surprise at the positive changes in spite of obstructions and difficulties generally. As two fathers wrote, 'in spite of the antagonism the children are happy and accepting of me' and 'we are closer together despite what happened'. The fathers who have overcome the difficulties refer to the qualities needed to keep the relationship alive and 'make it ordinary'. These are described as 'hard work', 'a lot of effort', 'the need for encouragement and support', and the need to plan one's life and think about how to use the limited time when in contact. There was a noticeable absence of such comments amongst the no-contact fathers.

When one looks at the difficulties over access certain obstacles are identical to those given by the no-contact fathers (see overleaf).

Although obstruction by the ex-wife is common to the two groups it was noticeable that many contact fathers were determined to overcome this difficulty. Such determination had clearly been an important factor in helping the father devise appropriate approaches when negotiating with the former partner.

	Number of times mentioned
Ex-wife's obstruction (either directly or indirectly)	13
Special difficulties of school holidays and unsuitable accommodation in which to meet	6
Time too short	4
Distance and cost	3
Access order which defines access and court welfare office arranges access	2
	28

We interviewed one remarried father who has struggled to keep in contact with his two young sons aged 11 and 10 since his divorce five years ago. He described his ex-wife's attitude towards him as vindictive and her behaviour towards the children as undermining him as their father. He felt he was fighting an 'uphill struggle' to remain in contact with his children and overcome the consequences of the undermining process. His dilemma was how to enforce his right and his wish to see his children without upsetting them and placing them in a difficult situation with their mother, and thereby causing more bitterness and problems. The strain of keeping in contact was evident, as he described the pressures on his health and work. However, he was determined not to lose contact and was prepared to take his case to court—as he had done once before to establish his right to defined access—if the obstruction worsened. His long-term view about retaining contact and continuing to be influential in his children's lives was not at all hopeful.

Contact and non-contact fathers compared As with other difficulties mentioned, contact fathers are able to be more precise about the problems of maintaining relationships and they often isolated specific problems. For example, there are four references to the shortness of time spent with their children, and three others to the exact financial costs involved and the difficulties brought about by long distances. This greater specificity in isolating factors fits in with one general theory about effective problem solving which suggests that a crucial element lies in the ability to break up the problem into smaller and more manageable components. The differences between the two groups are further emphasised when one looks at the comments which refer to the difficulties of maintaining the father role. Amongst the fathers in contact there are some references to 'not feeling like a proper father' and 'being more like an uncle' whose role is 'more that of material rather than emotional provider'. These are similar to some of the comments made by no-contact fathers. However, it is noticeable that amongst the no-contact group comments are expressed more crudely and in a more general form. This makes it more difficult to resolve the problem, and probably leads to a loss of belief that change is possible. In both groups the external obstacles to overcome are much the same and yet the outcomes are different. It would seem that the differences lie in how each group mobilises their inner and outer resources—how they manage their own feelings and needs and how they develop mechanisms for coping with loss and change in the face of external barriers.

We examined other attitudes and responses to see whether there were any differences between the two groups of fathers. For the purpose of these analyses the fathers who have children living overseas have not been included. The total size of the two groups is thus: 20 with no contact; 30 with contact. When we looked at the fathers' attitudes towards their ex-wives over access a clear differentiation emerged between the two groups. The following table shows the differences:

Attitude to ex-wife concerning access arrangements

	Friendly and middling	Unfriendly	Non-existent	Total
No-contact fathers	2	6	12	20
Contact fathers	16	11	3	30
Totals	18	17	15	50

Thus 90 per cent of the no-contact fathers assess their relationship as unfriendly or non-existent. When a relationship is judged to be non-existent it is clearly difficult to negotiate about access and thus the pattern of non-contact is likely to persist. In fact only three fathers had managed to remain in contact despite this problem. We learnt from the earlier analysis of the fathers' comments about difficulties over access that many fathers continued to have contact despite difficulties of obstruction by their ex-wife and this pattern is confirmed in this analysis since eleven fathers have remained in contact despite unfriendly relationships between the parents. By contrast, over half of the fathers in contact assess their relationship as friendly or middling. Evidently without encouragement from the children's mother it is much more difficult to maintain and develop the reciprocal father role.

Clear differences between the two groups also arise when one looks at the different assessments fathers make of changes in their relationship with their children. Eighty-five per cent of the no-contact fathers describe the relationship as having deteriorated compared with only 55 per cent of those in contact. Similarly with new mental health problems we found that all except one of the no-contact fathers have developed some kind of a mental health problem since the divorce. Other studies confirm these findings indicating that divorce and the need to redefine one's parental role spark off strong emotional reactions, some of which may not necessarily be directly related to the children. In our study anger generally and negative attitudes towards the ex-partner were the dominant emotions to be aroused. The term 'anger' covers a wide spectrum of emotions ranging from depression, guilt, shame and grief through to embitterment, rage and a sense of injustice. Whilst we were not able to differentiate between these emotions we were struck by the relationship between high anger levels and a failure to keep in contact with the children. Moreover the cost of not resolving these emotions often appears to have affected mental health and sometimes physical health as well.

As an example, one man we interviewed, who had been divorced for over two years, had experienced both physical ill health and a suspected 'heart attack' which proved negative after tests. He also reported mental health symptoms in the form of sleeplessness, a high level of non-specific anxiety and rapid changes of mood from 'cheerfulness' to 'resentment and bitterness'. He said that before the divorce he had not suffered any of these conditions. The effect of these various 'illnesses' has led him to review seriously the high personal emotional costs of keeping in touch with his two adolescent daughters. Although conclusions based on these comments must inevitably be tentative, it seems that to improve contact and relationship between fathers and their children, more thought needs to be given to helping fathers express their strongly-felt anger and negative attitudes and feelings. Wallerstein and Kelly found that it was in the period immediately after divorce that fathers were most appreciative of advice and they commented on '. . . how fluid the father-child relationship appeared'. Our evidence suggests that if the anger and negative feelings are not dealt with *at that point* they continue to persist and affect important aspects of the father's later relationship and contact with his children.

The issues facing visiting fathers Several commentators have described the effects of divorce on the individual as a 'little death' with none of the parties remaining untouched by the eventual outcome and each harbouring feelings about what went wrong to sour the original relationship. For fathers one aspect of the little death occurs with the sudden break in the pattern of regular contact with their children and the lose of familiarity in their relationship. The access visit symbolises the abrupt ending of the old ways of relating and emphasises much of what has been lost in the divorce. For some the shock is a sudden and immediate realisation that they must adapt to the time and physical limits of the access visits. Our study of all the fathers whose children were in the custody of their ex-wives shows the various ways in which they dealt with one aspect of this 'little death' and how they adapted to the changed circumstances in terms of the patterns of contact that have emerged. In our analysis we have identified some factors which differentiate the fathers who have maintained contact from those who have lost contact with their children. Higher levels of anger, stronger negative attitudes and a higher incidence of mental health problems characterise the no-contact fathers and distinguish them from those who keep in contact. These are important differences and affect, in turn, the probability of future contact.

However, the more striking finding is the *similarity* of the issues and problems facing all fathers seeking to keep in contact with their children. The differences are related to the ways fathers coped with and adapted to these rather than to the issues and problems themselves. We therefore decided to examine in more general terms why maintaining contact between visiting fathers and their children is problematic. The focal point of all contact is the meeting that takes place between the father and his child or children. What are the difficulties surrounding the meeting? We decided to look at those imposed by the *context* of the meeting and those that are *internally generated* by the feelings and reactions of the father.

(a) *Contextual difficulties* There are problems to do with the lack of preparation and experience for the meeting and the kind of encounter that can take place within the time limits and the context imposed on the participants. At a practical level fathers are faced with issues of where to meet, how to spend the time available and how frequently to meet. At another level they are faced with how to relate to their children—what to talk about, what to ask about, what to share of their own lives, and how to deal with their children's behaviour, particularly if it is difficult and emotionally charged. Because of the loss of the regular contact which allows for closer integration of the caring and controlling aspects of parenting, fathers have to consider how far they are able to discipline and how much affection to show to their children. Where fathers are fearful about losing their children's affection and esteem this may pose a major difficulty, particularly if the meeting occurs with a new partner present.

The time boundary sharpens the nature of the meeting, emphasising the coming together and separation in a way that is uncharacteristic of pre-divorce relationships. For some fathers, this time limitation may be welcomed as it provides an external boundary to the occasion, but for others the anticipation of parting at a fixed hour may dominate the meeting itself. Whatever the reaction, the limited time element is a constantly recurring feature of the meetings. For at least one father, the pain of parting was a major factor in deciding to break off contact altogether. The context of, and arrangements for, the meeting are also important. They provide possible opportunities for a reopening of old wounds and sore feelings between the parents. However fleeting the contact may be, when a father collects and returns his children to his ex-wife, there is always a chance the unresolved feelings will be recharged and exacerbated. For the many fathers in our study who have strongly felt negative attitudes towards their ex-wife and her new partner, it is hard to imagine these occasions passing uneventfully and easily.

The mother's feelings and attitudes towards her ex-husband over access and the relationship he has with the children also pose problems and may affect the meeting. These may be exacerbated if she also has angry and resentful feelings about dealing with the children's behaviour after a meeting with their father, and sees any subsequent difficulties in terms of the meeting and what the father might have said or done. The children's own attitudes and feelings towards meeting are another important and unavoidable issue.

Wallerstein and Kelly describe the 'children's yearnings for their fathers which not only continued but sometimes intensified in the years following the father's departure'. Sometimes these feelings may be tempered by their own need to cope with a sense of being in the middle and feeling responsible for the rows and arguments between their parents when they meet. In the same way the fathers fear the loss of their children, the same fears can be experienced by children who may respond by, for example, withdrawal or manipulative behaviour towards both parents.

(b) *Internal difficulties* The internal difficulties relate to the emotional problems facing fathers. Divorce itself involves coping with a failed relationship and the subsequent blow to the person's pride, self-esteem and self-identity. Where there are children involved fathers are faced with their feelings about the break-up, what they have done to their children, and how they might repair the damage. Some clearly become depressed, others feel very guilty, and others act out their angry feelings in a vindictive and revengeful manner. Rebuilding an unhinged identity and finding new sources for restoring damaged self-esteem are key internal issues facing all divorced fathers, and the way this process is handled is likely to affect the amount of contact and the kind of relationships between fathers and their children.

Faced with this array of possible constraints it is perhaps surprising that fathers and their children managed to meet at all, and yet thirty of our sample continued to be in contact and to build, with varying degrees of success, a new relationship as a visiting parent. The essential ingredients for fathers to defeat these varied constraints would seem to be an ability to find ways of overcoming the obstacles, both felt and actual; a preparedness to risk and tolerate a certain amount of abuse, hostility and ambivalent feelings; a capacity to manage one's own strong feelings and reactions in such a way that they do not reopen the old sores and keep the marital conflicts alive; and a willingness and imaginative capacity to work out new patterns of meeting, relating and communicating with their children.

In isolation it is unlikely that many fathers would be able to meet these expectations. For this reason positive support networks made up of friends, family, workmates and colleagues, or a combination of these, are essential both for survival and for learning new patterns of relating. Positive and active encouragement in maintaining contact and building a new relationship by the children's mother also seems to be important. From our evidence, discouraging attitudes and unco-operative behaviour by the mother clearly have a marked negative effect on the amount of contact and the quality of the new relationship. We have provided this identikit picture of the ideal ingredients for overcoming the constraints facing the visiting father not because we believe all men will be able to realise it but because we believe it may be helpful for fathers who are experiencing these difficulties to see more clearly the overall picture and to identify some of their own specific areas of difficulty. Our evidence of those who have maintained contact and rebuilt their relationships with their children is that it is demanding and stressful but often unexpectedly rewarding.

FATHERS WITH CUSTODY

There are eleven cases in all where the father is acting as a custodial parent. In eight of these the father was given the sole custody of the children; two other cases involve split custody with at least one child living with the father and in one instance there is a joint custody order with care and control of two children to the father and one child to the maternal grandparents. In one of the cases, three of the children of the marriage live with their father and two children by the ex-wife's first marriage live with her. In two other instances the children are now in their 20s and 30s but as they were much younger at the time of divorce they have been included because the fathers commented on the experience of sole parenting.

Taking all eleven cases together, there are twenty-three children involved. At the time of the divorce about half of these were 11 or over. There were also slightly more boys than girls living in the sole custody of the father. In seven of the cases the custody was not contested. In three cases where it was, one resulted in a joint custody order being made with care and control to the father, in another there was a split custody order and in the third the custody petition was dropped at the divorce. One father did not indicate whether or not custody was contested.

In the same way that we examined the amount of contact for non-custodial fathers, we also looked at how often visiting mothers had contacted their children in the past month. While the numbers were too small to draw any firm conclusions, there was a similar pattern to that for fathers; three had not visited at all, four visited occasionally and four were in frequent contact. We looked at how the fathers judged their relationship with their ex-wives over access, and the majority, seven, described it as either friendly or middling, and only four as either very unfriendly or non-existent.

We decided to look more closely at the ways in which having sole custody affected fathers by asking them to describe how they had changed as a direct result of having a larger share in the care of the children. Had they learned any new skills or made any new contacts? The comments made were as follows:

Effects on father	Number of times mentioned
Improved domestic skills	5
Social life reduced	4
No change	3
More social contacts	3
Feel more fulfilled/independent	2
Less money to spend	1
Appreciate women's problems more	1
Children act as a steadying influence	1
	20

Although there are more positive than negative changes mentioned they are mainly of a practical nature, whereas the negative ones refer to their changed social and emotional life.

We also asked about the specific ways in which relationships with the children had changed. The comments are shown below:

Changes in relationship	Number of times mentioned
Closer/more understanding relationship	6
Less tension/more relaxed	3
Children more reliant on father	2
Greater sharing of feelings and life styles	2
Hard work and effort to do all the jobs	2
Difficult to combine several roles	1
Feel I am more strict and protective	1
Tend to treat them more like adults	1
Tend to treat them more like friends	1
Children have benefitted educationally	1
Learned not to expect appreciation	1
Fear of being over-protective and over-compensating for absent mother	1
More stress at adolescence	1
Interference by mother	1
	24

At least fourteen of these twenty-four comments were clearly positive. On the other hand one man commented that one-parent families headed by a father are not very successful for either the children or the father. In the same way as visiting fathers have to learn to adapt to their new role, so it is with fathers with sole custody. Since only two of these eleven fathers had remarried, the comments also reflected the difficulties of acting as a single parent.

It is clear that having responsibility for the care of the children means that all fathers have to devote more time to them. One man we interviewed, who is now remarried and has the custody of his three adolescent children, talked about the amount of extra time and energy consumed in bringing up the children, particularly when they were younger. These pressures, he felt, would have seriously affected his work and career generally if his job had involved a greater strictness about time and availability. He was also concerned that in the day-to-day task of bringing up the children he would lose sight of their individual emotional and developmental needs. Eight of the eleven fathers comment on these strains which are also reflected in mentions of illnesses and the adverse changes in the mental health suffered by six of the eleven.

Although the group of sole custody fathers is very small it is noticeable how serious are the financial and career effects generally for most of them. Equally it needs to be noted that over half of them express positive changes in how they see themselves and, despite the extra work involved in bringing up children, describe positive changes in their relationships with them. Moreover most of them still maintain their original family and friendship network, although judging from some of the comments about the shortage of time it is doubtful whether many fathers have as much contact with their friends as they would like. There is only one father in the eleven who is very angry and bitter towards his ex-wife and this is a case of split custody. All the others, despite the costs to career and general financial position, and the demands on their time and energy, seem tolerably content with the situation. It may be that as the ex-wife is remarried or has another partner in eight of the cases the pressure and interference from her is considerably reduced, and it is therefore easier to adapt to the new role. Moreover in two of the cases where the former wife is not remarried she is described as being ill and permanently unable to be actively involved. Only one father mentioned his former wife's interference as a problem.

Effects on Work and Career

Everyone in the survey was asked: '*What effects do you think the break-up had on your work or career at the time?*' Five possibilities were suggested on the form and the answers were as follows:

	Number of men	Percentage
Very good effects	8	9
Fairly good effects	4	4
None at all	23	25
Serious effects	44	48
Disastrous effects	13	14
	92	100

Thus for nearly two-thirds of the sample the career consequences were judged to be serious or disastrous, a very considerable effect. The next question on the form went on to ask, of the fifty-seven who had indicated adverse effects, what specifically had caused the damage to their career prospects. The answers were as shown below.

Reason	Number of times stated
Changes in living arrangements	35
Changes in health	32
Need to spend more time with the children	16
Worried and unable to concentrate	6
Lost interest and motivation in work	4
Lost self-confidence	4
Financial worries	3
Extra time off to sort things out	2
General bitterness affecting work	2
Vindictive calls from ex-wife to employer	2
Employer's doubts about employing a divorcee	2
Anger at the Probation Service	1

Disruption of domestic arrangements clearly has a severe effect for most of the forty men who we found earlier had moved out of the matrimonial home. Almost as important were the changes in mental health which have been discussed earlier in this chapter. Of the ninety-two men, only eleven were acting as custodial fathers so the sixteen who mentioned the need to spend more time with the children as a factor affecting their career must include at least five who were living apart from their children but clearly devoted so much time to seeing them, or possibly moving to remain close to them, that they felt their careers had been affected.

Most of the reasons listed reflect feelings of worry, anger, or reduced ability to concentrate on work. For example, one man, a general practitioner, felt his work was affected by '. . . pre-occupation with my own problems when I was trying to help others', while another referred to '. . . the diversion of mental energy and time to dealing with legal matters'. Another felt that he was unable to function properly at work because his mind was constantly re-volving around what he regarded as '. . . the biased attitudes of the court welfare officer in the Probation Service'. Several others referred to bitterness at the injustice, as they saw it, of being blamed for something they had not brought about and they regarded these feelings as the reason for serious, or in some cases disastrous, effects on their capacity to work properly.

Other men referred to practical considerations which had led to severe disruption of their careers, such as the need to take consi-derable amounts of time off to see solicitors, Welfare Officers, etc. Others again referred to 'substantial debts' resulting from the divorce proceedings and one man, who previously ran a small shop and sub-Post Office, found it impossible to combine this activity with the care of the two children in his custody. He had been obliged to sell the property. Several men felt that their transition from married to divorced status had adversely affected their chances in the labour market. One (a police sergeant) wrote that he felt less acceptable socially and professionally while another felt that this employer was 'distrustful of divorced persons'. A final telling point was made by one man, a company director in his mid-30s, who felt that his motivation had been badly affected by the marriage break-up. He commented,

'I kept asking myself why I was bothering to build up a business'.

Ironically the same man had given 'my total involvement in my work' as the main reason for the break-up of the marriage.

The permanence, or otherwise, of the adverse effects on work is perhaps as important as the severity of the effect at the time. The question was therefore asked: '*Would you say that the adverse*

effects on your work, if any, were permanent or a thing of the past?'
To this the fifty-seven who had indicated adverse effects replied as
follows: permanent 22; a thing of the past 35. Taking the replies at
their face value, nearly a quarter of the total sample feel that their
careers have been permanently affected, either seriously or disastrously, by the break-up of their marriage. Given a million or so
divorces in the past decade this points to a large number of permanently affected careers—an effect important for the individuals
concerned, for the efficiency of organisations for which they work,
and ultimately, to some extent, for the economy as a whole.

For the purposes of analysis it seemed useful to combine the two
aspects of the *degree* of the effect and its *permanence* or otherwise
into a single indicator with which other factors could be compared.
This was done as follows:

Nature of career effect	Number of men
None, or a positive effect	35
Serious effects, now better	30
Disastrous effects, now better	5
Serious effects, permanent	14
Disastrous effects, permanent	8
	92

Thus nearly two fifths of the sample noted no adverse effects or
positive effects, the same proportion had been badly affected but
felt they had overcome the effects and roughly a fifth considered the
damage to be permanent. We attempted to sort out some of the
factors that produced these various effects.

One might expect that things would get better with time but
matters are not that simple. The eight who said the effects had been
disastrous and permanent had been divorced, on average, more
than four years ago and were still feeling that way. But the other
'disastrous' group, those who felt the effects were now quite over,
had been divorced only two and a half years on average. Clearly
some recover from a disastrous setback within a short time while
others still feel the effect after a much longer period and expect the
damage to continue indefinitely. From the level of questioning in
the survey it was impossible to sort out meaningful differences
between the two groups although the issue seems a very significant

one. The age at divorce seems to shed a limited, but systematic, light on the question in the sense that the older the person at divorce, the less the career damage (the disastrously and permanently damaged group were, on average, four and a half years younger than the unaffected group).

As might be expected, the degree of damage to career also depends to an extent on what sort of job the individual does:

Type of occupation	Percentage of the sample whose career was unaffected or benefited by the divorce
Professional	50
Intermediate non-manual	38
Junior non-manual	31
Skilled manual	30
Semi-skilled manual	16
Unskilled manual	0

Any number of possible explanations of this variation in career risk might be advanced. Non-manual jobs tend (or at any rate tended till recently) to be more secure, and employers to be perhaps more understanding about sick leave, time off to sort matters out and so on. Also, as a generalisation, work of this sort may well be more fulfilling and satisfying, or carry more responsibility, such that job satisfaction enables the individual better to overcome the hurt and stress associated with a marriage break-up.

It was thought that there might be some connection between the amount of help and advice offered over the crucial period and the extent of the subsequent damage to career prospects. So far as the sources of help and advice we identified are concerned, the expected pattern of more help equals reduced damage to career does not seem to occur at all. In fact there are some quite strong indications of a reverse relationship. The men who reported positive or no effects on their careers had sought help and advice somewhat *less* than the sample as a whole. Similarly the group suffering the most disastrous and permanent career effects seems to have consulted all sources of help somewhat more freely than the rest of the sample but to have found that, nevertheless, the damaging effects of the break-up could not be overcome. The conclusion seems to be that career damage cannot be attributed to any reluctance on the part of the individual to seek out sources of help and support. It occurs *despite* this. An equally significant conclusion is that many, perhaps most, men simply could not find the people and agencies to give them the help they needed. We feel that this strengthens the arguments for more effective support systems geared to the needs of men which we put forward in Chapter 9.

Adverse career effects seem to relate to the situation concerning the children, if any, in a number of ways. *All* those reporting permanent career damage have children. Of those without any children of custodial age, only 22 per cent reported damaging career effects whereas the percentage for those with custodial children was 72. The exception to these general trends was provided by two men who were acting as custodial fathers but who still felt their careers had benefitted from the break-up. One is a professional civil servant with three children and the other a farmer with two children (now above custodial age). Both remarried in the same year as the divorce. Despite these two rather special cases it is clear that the fathers in the survey who took on the task of rearing their children following a divorce did so, in the majority of cases, at the cost of long-lasting damage to their career prospects. This points (as it does in the case of single-parent women) to the need for better provision to help single-parent fathers with the care of their children while they carry on with their career.

The relationship between work effects and children does not end there. Fifty-five men in the sample had children of custodial age who were in the care of the ex-wife. A strong relationship was noticed between the frequency with which they visited their children and the extent to which they felt their career had been affected. The least career-damaged group visited, on average, 2.7 times per month and the worst affected group visited only 0.7 times per month. The evidence is not conclusive because of the unmeasured effects of other factors (such as distance from the children) but it does seem possible that career-damaged fathers might have some inhibitions about keeping in close touch with their children, possibly because in some cases they feel they might have lost the respect of their children by failing to advance their careers or even by having lost their job. This, if true, would be a doubly serious effect of marriage break-up.

Changes in health following a divorce show a very clear relationship with the reported degree of career damage. Only 17 per cent of the least career-damaged group reported new serious mental health difficulties whereas the percentage for those declaring permanent career-damage was 59. In fact all eight men who declared their careers to be disastrously and permanently damaged also reported new severe mental health problems although, as always when confronted only with the answers at this level of simplicity, no assessment can be made of which effect 'caused' which. A similar effect, somewhat less clear, is evidenced by the pattern of new physical ailments. The incidence of such illness tends to increase steadily as the degree of career damage rises. This pattern is interrupted by one curious and possibly significant feature. Of the five men who said that the damage had been disastrous at the time but was now a thing of the past, four had suffered new physical illnesses since the divorce (for the most part such stress-related ailments as severe headaches, chest pains, blackouts, fainting fits and liver problems brought on by drinking). As has been noted earlier, the career recovery of this group has been surprisingly rapid since they had been divorced an average of only two-and-a-half years. Possibly this indicates that although they may have felt that the adverse effects had been overcome in *career* terms, there was still a price to be paid, in terms of ill-health, for what had happened.

Remarriage (and presumably other stable new relationships not recorded in the survey) seems to be associated with lesser degrees of career damage. Of those who had remarried, 88 per cent reported that their career had benefitted or received no worse than temporary damage as a result of the break-up. For the non-remarried this figure was only 62 per cent. Similarly, of the 'disastrously' career damaged group only 14 per cent had remarried; of the rest, 31 per cent had done so.

The strongest common factor linking all three issues of career, contact with children and remarriage may well be the changes in self-image experienced after a break-up. These changes are discussed in much greater detail in Chapter 8 but for the moment it can be noted that negative changes in self-image are closely associated with high levels of career damage. There was an equally clear tendency for positive changes in self-image to be associated with lesser degrees of career damage—over half of those who felt strongly positive changes in their personality as a whole also reported very positive effects on their work and only one reported any permanent adverse effects on his career.

As a final step we decided to see what could be said of the group (twelve in all) who felt that the break-up had been *beneficial* for their careers. Over half of these had remarried (as compared to only 24 per cent of the rest) and the majority were working in occupational class 2—that is, fairly skilled non-manual work not carrying 'professional' status. The group with beneficial career effects had been divorced, on average, longer than the rest, they had been married longer, and they were, on average, older when divorced. These findings are mildly surprising and possibly indicate that a number of long-established marriages were, towards the end, producing tensions which were having bad effects on work and which, on divorce, were eased leading to a beneficial effect.

Only four of the group of twelve had children of custodial age so it is difficult to draw any conclusions about the relationship between beneficial career effects and children except to say that having no children under 16 appears to give a much better chance of enjoying such beneficial effects after divorce. It is, perhaps, worth noting that the three men with younger children who reported 'very good' career effects visited their children, on average, nearly four times more frequently than did fathers as a whole. The group reporting beneficial career effects was also characterised by a low incidence of new severe mental health problems (only two of the twelve). There was also an important connection with the assessment made of overall personality change; ten of the twelve felt positively about the overall change in themselves since divorce, whereas of the group with damaged careers, only about 36 per cent had anything positive to say about the change in their lives. The reverse was also true. In fact only four of the total sample of ninety-two men had experienced *either* disastrous career effects combined with positive feelings about personality change *or* the reverse—positive career effects combined with generally negative feelings about the change in their personality.

Effects on Financial Position

Since the break-up of a marriage is obviously likely to have considerable effects on a man's financial position, the question was put: '*In which ways, if any, would you say that your financial position had been seriously affected by the break-up and divorce?*' Four possible ways were suggested on the form and a space was left for 'other'. The answers were as shown on the table set out on the next page.

Adverse effect	Number of men mentioning this effect
Serious loss of capital assets	52
Cost of divorce proceedings	38
Maintenance or other payments to ex-wife	36
Earning capacity reduced as a direct result of the break-up	28
Unable to make joint plans	3
Extra housing costs	3
Loss of solely owned assets	2
Failure of the court to supervise arrangements	2
Cost of boarding school	1
Cost of access proceedings	1
Travel costs to see children	1
Own business collapsed	1
Loss of life insurance interest	1

The first four reasons were listed on the form and produced a sizeable response. It seems likely that had the latter nine reasons also been listed some of them would have been stated more frequently.

Some of the amplifying comments gave a good idea of the range and variety of the possible financial effects. At one extreme was the man in his late 20s (whose marriage had been childless) who commented: 'I'm ten times better off, she used to spend money like water' and at the other the man in his mid-50s who had been married for twenty-four years and who apparently had needed to sell all the investments left to him by his father, and to use all his own cash resources, to pay legal costs and make a lump sum payment to his wife. As he commented; '. . . she took me to the cleaners'. This man also felt strongly that all solicitors are 'hand in glove' with each other. He reported that he had made this point to his solicitor:

I said if you are fighting my case I don't want you drinking with him in the evening after sending him [ie. her solicitor] strongly worded letters.

In the end, although no custody issue arose, he paid 'several hundred pounds' legal fees and £500 towards the costs. Another man (the investment manager of a merchant bank!) drew attention to the difficulties of making financial decisions alone:

Whereas a married couple can discuss which items of expenditure are to be reduced if money is short, a divorced couple cannot. . . .

Two men in the sample, by their determination to secure what they regarded as an appropriate outcome, got into very lengthy and costly litigation. One, after five years of legal wrangling and episodes such as the removal of his only daughter to America by the ex-wife and boy friend, has finally achieved the outcome he wanted. This has entailed converting the matrimonial home into two flats, one of which was sold to release capital to the ex-wife. It was also necessary to take out a second mortgage, at considerable expense, to supplement the capital payment he had to make. The outcome is that the daughter, now 14 and a ward of court, lives for one-third of the year in her old bedroom in his flat, thus keeping contact with childhood friends and neighbours.

The second man, divorced nine years ago, has spent the last seven years seeking to combat a court order preventing his access to his daughter following a disputed custody case. Alleging that the ex-wife and her solicitor had committed perjury, he took the matter to the European Court of Human Rights but so far has been successful only in having maintenance payments reduced to a nominal £12 per year. He still has not seen his daughter and the expense of the litigation has used up all his share of the capital from the sale of the former matrimonial home.

Some of these financial effects are clearly 'once and for all', for example the cost of legal proceedings (although it probably does not feel that way to the doctor in the sample who is paying off his legal costs over twenty-five years—we found that payment by instalment is by no means uncommon). Other costs, such as the temporary loss of a fully proportionate share in property assets and reduced earning capacity related to the career effects discussed above, may have a longer-lasting or even life-long effect. As in the case of assessing career effects, the problem was to simplify matters by producing one single indicator of financial impact which combined, as accurately as possible, both the 'capital' and the 'revenue' costs of a divorce settlement. This was done by noting the presence or absence of the first four financial effects mentioned above, taking into account the effects of 'other' forms of financial loss, and including in the assessment any written comments concerning the seriousness of the financial impact that may have been made. By this means we arrived at the following breakdown by degrees of financial impact. The grouping procedure, while to some extent arbitrary, does seem to reflect the reality in a reasonable fashion and it enables

Degree of financial effect	Number of men
Nil or very minor	20
Significant	23
Serious	35
Severe	11
Extremely severe	3
	92

further study to be carried out. The groupings also corresponded well with the 'career effects' groupings (also on a scale of five) because 73 per cent of the sample registered either the same number on both scales or just one number different.

There was a clear connection between the stated severity of the financial impact and the length of time since the divorce. Those reporting nil or very minor effects had been divorced, on average, nearly six-and-a-half years whereas those suffering extremely serious effects averaged only just over two years since their divorce. This seems to indicate either that financial settlements are becoming tougher for men, or that the passing of time lessens the actual or perceived severity of the effects. The extent of the financial loss seems to bear no relationship to the age at which the divorce occurred or to the length of the marriage (which is a little surprising), but there is some evidence that it is related to the type of job done with a tendency for skilled manual and lower skilled clerical workers to be affected more seriously than any other groups.

There is also a clear relationship between the degree of financial loss and the pattern of help-seeking at the time of the divorce. Those who sought help most actively, whether from friends and neighbours or more formal agencies, had on the whole suffered much more serious financial effects. This seems to indicate that the expectation, or the reality, of severe financial problems considerably increases the probability of consultation with others—an effect similar to that noted when considering effects on career. The only other explanation, presumably less likely, is that consultation *itself* worsens the financial effect (although the evidence shows that in some cases this is a reasonable supposition when considering legal consultation as a form of help-seeking).

Financial loss is related quite strongly to health impairment, both mental and physical. Only one-fifth of the financially unaffected group experienced new physical illnesses since the divorce whereas double this proportion of those more seriously affected financially had suffered some new physical ailment. The same effect is evident with mental health difficulties. Of those reporting no adverse financial effects, 60 per cent also reported no mental health problems. But as the degree of financial loss increases so does the incidence of new mental illness so that only three of the fourteen most affected financially remained free of mental health problems. Obviously in this very complex situation, with many additional factors to be considered, it is impossible to make any statements about what 'causes' what, but certainly a strong relationship exists between financial loss and the incidence of ill-health following divorce.

Financial effects are also bound up with children in a variety of ways. Of those with no children, 63 per cent reported nil or very minor financial effects following divorce. The corresponding figure for those with children v/as 13 per cent. But when the group of custodial fathers (eleven in all) was compared with those fathers not having any custodial responsibilities it was rather surprisingly found that, on average, the fathers *with* custody reported slightly less serious financial losses than the rest. This is in sharp contrast to the point made earlier in the chapter that taking on the parenting role almost always resulted in serious career damage. The difference between the degree of career damage and the extent of financial loss probably results from a number of factors, such as the greater chance of the custodial father retaining the matrimonial home while receiving certain state benefits and remaining free of maintenance payments. In contrast to these various effects concerning children, remarriage by the man seems to have no discernable effect on the incidence of financial loss. Presumably the remarriage of the ex-wife may have some effect in the cases where the husband was helping to support her, but no questions were asked about this.

There are quite complicated relationships between financial loss, attitude towards the ex-wife, judgments about the fairness of the financial outcome, and feelings about the personality changes that had resulted from the break-up. When asked: '*Overall, do you feel that the financial arrangements now in operation, between yourself and your former wife are . . .?*' the answers were as shown overleaf:

Very fair	21 }	39
Quite reasonable	18	
Rather unreasonable	10 }	29
Very unfair	19	

(In twenty-four cases the settlement had not yet been finalised or no answer was given.)

This gives the impression that a tolerably fair financial outcome has occurred in the majority of cases. But concealed beneath this is a clear relationship between financial loss and general feelings towards the ex-wife. Of the group suffering nil or very minor financial loss, 43 per cent have remained on some kind of a friendly basis with their ex-wife. This percentage declines rapidly as the degree of financial loss increases until of the fourteen men worst affected financially, none remains in a friendly relationship with the ex-wife. It is impossible to detect whether the severity of the loss governs the attitude or whether divorce settlements amicably arrived at and maintained tend to be less hard on the man (in his own view). There appears also to be a strong relationship between the extent of financial loss and the overall assessment, positive or negative, of the personality changes that have occurred since the break-up (see Chapter 8). Of the fourteen most severely affected financially, only two felt any degree of positive change when asked the question: '*In what important ways do you feel you have changed as a person as a result of the break-up?*' By contrast, over half of those less severely affected financially felt that the changes in their life had been, on balance, positive. This seems to indicate that self-assessment, which may be another way of expressing self-respect, is tied to changes in one's financial position in important ways.

Effects on Patterns of Friendship

The ending of a marriage very often has profound effects on the pattern of friendships especially in relation to the friends the divorcing couple knew mutually over the period when they operated socially as a pair. No matter how solid such friendships may feel when affairs are progressing 'normally', various unpredictable and hurtful consequences can result when the marriage founders and friends find they have to deal not with the familiar sociable pair, but with two unhappy people going their separate ways. The resultant situation, probably with each partner blaming the other and each appealing to the same mutual friend for support, can stretch resourcefulness and tact to the limit. Even if neither of the divorcing pair is placing any direct blame for the break-up on a particular friend (although anecdotal evidence seems to suggest that most instances of adultery concern a mutual friend), there is still often a general temptation, when badly hurt, to misinterpret the intended helpful acts of friends. It is easy to place unreasonable demands upon them or to imagine, when total support is not forthcoming, that the friends have 'taken sides' in favour of the ex-partner.

To these difficulties must be added, in many cases, the embarrassment, defensiveness and the '. . . there but for the grace of God go I . . .' feelings with which many receive the news of the break-up of friends' marriages. Most people grew up in times before the 1971 legislation and the growth of the critical women's literature on marriage. Even fifteen or twenty years ago divorce was far more rare and, in terms of public opinion, far more shocking than it is now. All these factors can sometimes combine to produce a situation in which friends tend to make the right general noises about '. . . now you are on your own we must go out for a drink/invite you round for a meal . . .' but to be slow in issuing actual invitations. Even when they do, it was evident from many comments that some men lived in isolated worlds partly of their own making. One wrote:

I decline most invitations to parties or other gatherings where everybody else has a partner.

The survey sought to assess the effects of divorce on friendship networks by asking the question:
'*Of the set of mutual friends you had when you were married, are you now as close to . . .?*' The pattern was as follows:

	Number of men
To all of them	5
To most of them	24
To about half of them	8
To a few of them	26
To none of them	26
No answer	3
	92

Clearly for well over half the sample (about 56 per cent) the previous network of mutual friends had been badly affected or had collapsed altogether. Unfortunately no information was gathered about the effect on friendships that *pre-date* the marriage but it is difficult to imagine that these would re-flower to a sufficient extent to balance the loss of mutual friends and to counter the inhibitions and caution many feel about forming new, post-divorce, friendships. The clear conclusion is that for many, perhaps most, divorce is an isolating experience in more ways than one.

The survey form also asked:
'How many of these friends do you think "took sides"?'
To this the answers were:

All	3
Most	25
About a half	15
A few	26
None	17
No answer	6
	92

The sixty-nine men who did feel that mutual friends had 'taken sides' felt that these partisan feelings were divided as follows:

Most supported me most	30
Most supported my former wife most	20
Evenly balanced	19
	69

Taken together, these answers seem to reflect a reasonably even-handed set of reactions by mutual friends and do not, in themselves, provide anything like enough reason for the near-decimation of the mutual friendship network noted earlier. Perhaps more of the explanation is grounded in the reluctance, lack of confidence, or whatever, of the individual *himself* to maintain friendships. Perhaps the predominant instinct in many is for a change of scene—a withdrawal from the pattern of friendship and social life built up as one of a married pair.

It is possible to offer some comment on the relationship between changes in the friendship network and other factors that might possibly help in understanding them. Quite surprisingly, remarriage had no discernable effect on the overall pattern of changes in friendships built up in the previous marriage. For the sample as a whole, such friendships were equally likely to be maintained whether one remarried or not. But it is possible that this neutral effect is in fact the net result of two separate effects. Remarriage may, in some cases, finally sever the old pattern of first marriage friendships; in other cases it may represent a return to 'normality'—one can look up old friends again from the more secure basis of a new marriage, rejoin the 'pairs' scene and take pleasure in introducing a new wife to lapsed, but valued, friends.

Occupational class appears to have little effect on the survival of friendship networks except that both professional and skilled manual workers had maintained a higher proportion of their old friendships than had other groups. The post-divorce residential arrangements had a more marked effect. Of the fifty-two men who had moved out of the former matrimonial house, only nine, or 17 per cent, had maintained more than half of their former friendships; the corresponding figure for men who stayed in the matrimonial home was 54 per cent. There is also an evident connection between the attitude held towards the ex-wife and the survival of the mutual friendship network:

Attitude to ex-wife	Percentage maintaining half or more of former friendships
Very friendly	100
Quite friendly	69
Indifferent	41
Quite hostile	36
Very hostile	25

Probably the main explanation for these apparently similar attitudes and behaviour towards both ex-wife and friends lies in facets of the individual personality which could not be explored by the survey methods used. One clue may be provided by the interpretation offered of the way the support of friends was divided between the two parties. Of the thirty men who felt that friends' support, on the whole, was in their favour, fifteen still maintained close relationships with over half their former friendships. But only one man of the twenty who felt the ex-wife had received most support still kept up friendships to this extent.

It might be expected that the length of the marriage, the age at divorce and the length of time since the divorce might have helped to explain the survival of friendship patterns. In fact the length of the marriage does appear to have some effect since those maintaining over half their former friendships had been married, on average, nearly three years longer than the rest. Age at divorce had no effect on the question at all. But the length of time since the divorce does have an effect since the group maintaining half or more of their friendships had been divorced, on average, less than three and a half years; those who had 'lost touch' to a greater extent had been divorced on average five years.

Effects on Relationships with Parents and In-Laws

The question was put: '*As a result of the break-up, do you feel your relationship with your parents has become . . .?*' to which the answers were:

	Number
Much closer	15
A little closer	10
Much the same	36
A little more distant	2
Much more distant	5
	68
No answer or deceased	24
	92

It did not seem, therefore, that divorce had led to serious estrangements from parents. This pattern is not especially affected by factors such as occupational class, whether or not remarried, etc., nor is there much to distinguish the group of seven reporting *more distant* relationships with their parents except that six of the seven had experienced various mental health problems, and all of them were non-manual workers.

Changes in contact with former in-laws were somewhat more spectacular. To the question: '*Compared to before the break-up, do you now see your former in-laws . . .?*' the answers were:

	Number
Much more frequently	0
A little more frequently	2
As before	3
A little less frequently	2
Much less frequently	10
Never	62
	79
No answer or deceased	13
	92

Given the attitude most in-laws probably took as the marriage entered its rocky stage, these results are not surprising. It is nevertheless sad in that the relationship between children of the marriage and their maternal grandparents may well be badly affected by the failed relationship between their father and his former in-laws, especially so of course if he is the custodial parent. Furthermore, if the ex-wife has an equally distant relationship, after the divorce, with the man's parents, they too are likely to experience a saddening loss of contact with the children in the custody of their former daughter-in-law. This speculation raises an issue of some importance which seems not to have been adequately considered; the impact of the rapid rise in divorce on grandparent/grandchild relationships and, more generally, on the traditional three generational family structure.

The Combined Effects

We have looked at various effects of divorce in this chapter. Naturally the severity of the impact, whether in relation to money, health, career or relationship with children, varies a great deal among the ninety-two men. We did notice, however, that the effects were often interlinked. Men who had been badly affected in one way had often felt a very bad effect in several others. The reverse was also true; some men reported very little adverse effect in any area of their life.

It was therefore decided to combine the various effects into a single assessment: to identify a group of men *least* affected and a group *most* affected and to see what other characteristics each group had. Earlier in the chapter we assessed the impact of the marriage break-up in terms of changes in mental health, effects on career or employment, on financial position, and on friendship networks. Each of these had been assessed, for each respondent, on a five-point scale with one point denoting a negligible or even positive effect and five points denoting very severe effects. It was a simple matter to add up these scores for each of the ninety-two men and to identify a 'least affected' group with low total scores and a 'most affected' group with high total scores. The following summary shows some of the other characteristics of these two groups.

	The least affected group	The most affected group
Employment	Nearly all were in non-manual jobs	A high proportion of manual workers, few of them skilled
Children	None of this group had any children of custodial age	Nearly all had children of custodial age
Relationship to own parents	All reported unchanged relationships	Relationships to parents mostly changed — either much closer or more distant
Feelings about change in oneself (discussed more fully in Chapter 8)	Nearly all either positive or at worst neutral	Heavily negative; only one felt at all positive about himself

One of the surprising findings earlier in the chapter was that there seem to be very few signs of any 'recovery' process in that the adverse effects of the break-up on such aspects of life as friendship patterns, career, etc. were not getting better over time. Exactly the same finding emerged when comparing, for all ninety-two men, the extent of the combined effects with the number of years since the divorce. The graph made by plotting the two values against each other is not worth reproducing because it shows absolutely no trend at all. *In other words, men divorced very recently were just as likely to show high (or low) combined effects on their lives as men divorced ten or twenty years ago.* This cannot be taken as conclusive evidence that things do not, in fact, get better over time. To be certain about this we would need to document and assess the changes over time for each individual man rather than compare, collectively, the experience of many men in relation to the length of time since their divorce. Moreover a properly random sample rather than one based on self-selection would have been a surer basis. Nevertheless, the findings are suggestive, perhaps significant, and certainly rather disturbing. The clear implication is that the 'damage' in four very important areas of life that results from, or accompanies, a marriage break-up is not temporary. It is, as far as we can ascertain from our findings, quite likely to be permanent.

Chapter 8
Changed Attitudes

In the previous chapter we discussed the many and varying effects of a marriage break-up. For some men, a divorce is clearly a happy release. But for others the event represents the near collapse of a whole life-style—loss of a partner, the partial loss of role as a father, the collapse of friendship networks, serious disruption to career and financial position, and significant ill-health. The changes brought about, whether seen on balance as positive or negative, are bound to have effects on personality, values and outlook. We decided to study these changes in relation to four specific issues: changes experienced in oneself, changes in attitude to women, to remarriage and to the current state of matrimonial law. Finally we tried to assess how much anger was still felt by the men in the survey and to see whether this anger seemed to be lessening over time.

Changes in Self

We asked the question: '*In what important ways do you feel you have changed as a person as a result of the break-up?*' Answers ranged from the single word 'wrecked' to 'I feel free'. The main themes, grouped as 'generally negative' or 'generally positive', are as shown below.

It may be significant that the three most frequent negative statements, and the two most frequent positive ones, all seem to mark a turning inward, a movement away from dependence and/or connection with others towards self-sufficiency and isolation. Seen positively this is expressed as feelings of self-confidence, independence or self-awareness. For example, one man commented:

I feel that I am a happier and more self-confident person now and that I am much more in touch with my own needs.

But seen negatively it is often summed up as shyness, introversion and even alienation as is shown in the comments after the tables.

Generally negative	Number of times comment made
More bitter/less trusting	15
More shy/introverted/lonely	9
Feel strongly against the system/unpatriotic	7
More irritable/less tolerant	6
More insecure/worse at relationships	6
More pessimistic/lost interest in the future	6
Less confident	5
Worried and upset more easily	5
Sadder	2
More indecisive	2
More variable/unreliable	2
Less sense of humour	1
Self-neglectful	1
Mildly agoraphobic	1
	68

Generally positive	Number of times comment made
More confident/independent/optimistic	23
More in touch with myself	15
Happier/calmer	12
More mature/wiser	9
More easy-going/tolerant	7
Better able to relate/more considerate	6
More sociable	4
Less naive	3
Feel relieved and free	3
Realise attitudes and beliefs can change	2
More confident sexually	2
Less dogmatic	1
More reflective/questioning	1
Enjoy women's company more	1
	89

One man wrote:

I have become more isolated, probably more guarded . . . I do not know how I would react to a new relationship and whether I would drop my defences.

and another:

I tend to live within myself more—possibly more selfish—I *know* how much or how little I can rely on myself.

It is quite possible that in some men (and of course some women) these feelings were already gaining strength before the break-up, and simply could not be accommodated within the context of marriage as socially defined at present, or as they had defined it for themselves. In other cases the feelings may have grown (and been evaluated as 'positive' or 'negative') as the necessary adjustment to a move from married to non-married status.

Several other strong strands of meaning emerge from the comments. Many men commented on their increased awareness of the range of behaviour possible by their fellow human beings and of a consequent redefinition in their minds of the idea of 'humanity'.

I have been forced to modify my attitude to people . . . which hitherto consisted of giving them too much 'benefit of the doubt' i.e. I was assuming that their humanity was nearer the surface than in fact it often is. I have not become cynical but much more discriminating.

Another comment shows simultaneously how views on social relationships can change and how confusing these relationships can be:

I am sadder but really no wiser . . . I feel more isolated and more incapable of initiating and/or maintaining a mutually good relationship than before . . . . There seem to be rules to the game I never suspected . . . . I am much less naive than before.

Although the variety of negative and positive statements is identical the latter outnumber the former. If therefore seems, despite all the emotional and other stresses involved in the break-up, that there are clear benefits in personal terms for many in the sample. To indicate the balance of positive and negative changes we sorted each respondent into one of five groups based on the general tenor of his answer to the question and the result is set out on the next page.

When comparing these feelings with other factors that might possibly be important in helping to explain them it was found that the length of time since the divorce was not related in any way so there is no evidence that individuals go through a 'bad patch' in terms of

	Number
Entirely positive feelings	19
Mostly positive feelings	21
Mixed/neutral feelings	15
Mostly negative feelings	21
Entirely negative feelings	16
	92

self-evaluation and then gradually recover. Nor did the length of the marriage have any effect. Age seems to have some bearing on the issue since the present average age of the group reporting entirely positive changes was nearly four years younger than the rest.

The circumstances in which the marriage broke up seem to have a lasting effect in several ways. For example, of the men petitioners over half feel positive changes on balance. Where both partners petitioned over two-thirds feel positively but where the wife petitioned fewer than one-third of the men feel any positive change in their personality. Similarly, the group who stayed in the matrimonial home feel rather more positively about the way they have changed than do the group who left their home. Clearly in relation to both these factors there is some connection between positive feelings and the sense that one was exerting some control over one's destiny.

Feelings of rancour about the break-up itself have a very strong relationship to changes in self-image:

	Feelings towards ex-wife about why the marriage failed	
	Neutral or better	Blaming or recriminatory
Positive feelings about personal change	27	13
Negative feelings about personal change	9	28

There is also a close relationship between the general attitude to the ex-wife (which itself is closely related to feelings about the break-up) and feelings about changes in oneself. Of the eighteen men who still feel very hostile to their ex-wife, thirteen feel negative about the changes in themselves and only one feels positive. The indications are that anger at another person in this specific context often coincides with a more generalised anger at oneself in a way that can hardly be helpful to positive self-evaluation.

These linked feelings of anger and negative change seem to tie up closely with changes in mental health. In general those who had experienced new mental health problems were very much more likely to feel negatively about themselves. In fact almost all those expressing only negative feelings about the change in their lives had experienced mental ill-health. Negative feelings are also related to the reported impact of the marriage break-up on career and financial position, but to differing degrees. Of the forty-three men reporting least *financial* disadvantage following the divorce, twenty-four (56 per cent) saw positive changes in themselves whereas of the forty-nine men more seriously affected financially, only sixteen (32 per cent) felt any positive changes. The relationship to changes in *career* is more striking:

	Career effects	
	Positive or neutral effects	Adverse effects
Positive feelings about personal change	18	4
Negative feelings about personal change	7	14

Generally speaking, the research shows that feelings about changes in personality are bound up with other factors in a highly consistent way. The men who consider the changes to be negative are largely those who tend to blame their ex-wife for the break-up, who still harbour strongly hostile feelings towards her, who tend to have a much greater incidence of mental health problems and whose financial and, especially, career positions have been most severely affected.

Changes in Attitude to Women

It might be expected that the experience of a failed marriage would affect a man's subsequent attitude and approach to other women. It soon became apparent not only that this was true but also that the experience had led to a wide range of different conclusions about the opposite sex. These ranged from:

. . . [I] refuse to be a doormat, I am at long last standing up for my rights against the trained battalions of feminists

to:

. . . I find more pleasure in the company of women . . .

to:

. . . I have become more interested in the problems of women in society . . .

to:
    Much more sensible to my new girl friend, I'm more considerate and do not play around no more. I'm very happy.

The survey form included the question: '*How do you feel the break-up affected your approach to other women?*' and asked for an answer in terms of three different aspects of relationship; trust, confidence and sexual interest. The pattern of answers differed considerably among the three:

	'Trusting'		'Confident'		'Sexual interest'	
Much more	2 ⎫	4%	13 ⎫	33%	17 ⎫	40%
A little more	2 ⎭		16 ⎭		19 ⎭	
No change	19		20		28	
A little less	26 ⎫	75%	17 ⎫	45%	16 ⎫	29%
Much less	43 ⎭		24 ⎭		10 ⎭	

From these figures it appears that the average divorced man has to reconcile some rather mixed feelings as he seeks out new friends of the opposite sex; he is somewhat more rapacious, somewhat less confident and extremely mistrustful. If this set of feelings were to be reflected among divorced women (although we are unaware of any research on the subject) it seems reasonable to assume that the group dynamics of mixed clubs for the separated and divorced are both highly complex and highly charged.

    We analysed separately each of these three dimensions of feelings to see if any clear connections existed with other factors.

(a) *Trust*. Perhaps understandably, the most profound change in attitude concerns the readiness to place trust in new women friends. This constitutes a minor problem for the analysis because while sixty-nine speak of reduced readiness to trust, only four are more ready to be trusting. However, by combining the nineteen 'no change' men with these four, two groups of reasonable size were formed. We then identified some of the differences between the two groups. Certain factors seem to have no bearing on the matter. These include whether or not the man was the petitioner and whether or not he was the one to move out of the matrimonial home. Neither does age, the length of the marriage or the length of time since the divorce seem of any relevance.

Other factors are, however, strongly related. Of those who remain on tolerably amicable terms with their ex-wife, only 47 per cent have a generally less trusting attitude to women. Of those more strongly hostile to her, 86 per cent have acquired (or perhaps already had) mistrustful attitudes to women in general. Both these general feelings are probably related to the amount of blame attributed to the ex-wife for the break-up since, in rough terms, the degree to which mistrustfulness was expressed is related to the degree of blame put upon the former partner. The same sort of connection exists in relation to friendships generally: of the 'much less trusting towards women' group, nearly 75 per cent had lost touch with most of their former mutual friends, the corresponding figure for the rest of the sample was only 45 per cent. A greater proportion of career-damaged men have developed mistrustful attitudes than those whose careers were not damaged (83 as against 62 per cent) and the same general relationship holds good in relation to financial loss: four-fifths of the financially damaged men are now less trusting compared to three-fifths of those not affected in this way.

Perhaps the strongest relationship lies between the readiness to trust women and changes in mental health. Half of those with no new mental health problems have maintained their readiness to trust women whereas of those with such problems only 12 per cent still do so. Finally, it would be pleasant to imagine that remarriage and 'the love of a good woman' would tend to restore one's trust in the sex generally. Unfortunately this appears not to be so since the twenty-six men who have remarried (although in a sense voting with their feet in doing so) show negligible differences from the rest in this respect. This may indicate that many second marriages may have been built on realism and wariness rather than on a complete willingness to trust.

(b) *Confidence*. It was noted that twenty-nine men in the sample now approached women with more confidence and forty-one with less. This difference does not seem to relate in any noticeable way to who sought the divorce or how strongly the man now feels that the break-up was regrettable and/or not his fault. Nor is there much connection with the feelings a man now has for his ex-wife, although there is a slight tendency for those who are indifferent or hostile in feelings towards her to have lost confidence somewhat more than the rest. Remarriage appears to have no effect one way or the other.

Three factors do seem to bear on the matter. The 'much more confident' men are, on average, about four years older than the less confident men and (a factor which is closely related) they had been married noticeably longer. There was, however, no evidence that confidence returned over time following the divorce—in fact the less confident men had been divorced, on average, slightly longer than the rest. The second factor is the linked one of changes in career and financial position. Those most affected in these respects are far more likely than the rest of the sample to show a loss of confidence towards women.

Finally, changes in mental health correlate quite strikingly with changes in confidence levels since 58 per cent of men reporting new mental health problems had lost some confidence in their approach to women as against only 30 per cent of the rest.

(c) *Sexual Interest.* It is noticeable that this is the respect in which the most 'positive' changes occur in attitudes to women. About 40 per cent of the sample declared a greater sexual interest in women following their divorce as opposed to 29 per cent declaring less. As one man wrote:

For the first time in my life I am confident sexually,

while another declared:

I have celebrated my sexuality.

It is, however, very difficult to draw a clear picture of other factors which correlate with these changes in feelings. There is no relationship to age, length of marriage or period since divorce. Events surrounding the break-up seem to have some slight effect since men who were themselves petitioners, but who tended to accept reasonable amounts of blame and to hold fairly friendly attitudes to their ex-wife, tend to have gained rather than lost sexual interest.

Changes in mental health colour the attitude to some extent since

55 per cent of those free of mental health problems now show greater sexual interest as opposed to only 30 per cent of those with such problems. On the other hand, retention of the former network of friends is correlated only very weakly (if positively) with the retention of sexual interest so it does not seem that interest in new sexual relationships and general sociability are closely related. Remarriage seems to have no effect either way although it was probably especially difficult for remarried men to interpret the meaning of the question. Altogether the research identified no explanation why some men renew their sexual interest in women and some do not. It seems that the factors that might help to explain why sex once again rears its ugly head, or fails to do so, are too subtle and complex to be isolated by the research procedures used.

Certain points can be made to summarise the discussion of changes in attitude to women. The changes are sharply different for each of the three aspects of feelings. So too are the various factors that seem to correspond with, if not to explain, the changes. It is mildly surprising that, again, there is no evidence at all that any of the attitudes vary according to length of time since the divorce. There is no sign of either softening or hardening of feelings over time. Certain factors, such as the degree of blame, and the corresponding hostility, attached to the ex-wife, seem to correlate fairly consistently with the new attitudes that have been formed towards women while other such as changes in career and financial position affect certain subsequent attitudes towards women more strongly than others.

The factor that seems to correlate most strongly with the changes in attitude to women is the degree to which mental health problems have been experienced. The group most affected by such problems appear far less ready to trust women and, on average, they are much less confident in their approach to them. But even this factor seems less closely associated with reduced sexual interest. It is impossible to determine whether there is a 'third factor' explaining both the incidence of mental ill-health *and* changes in trust and confidence, or alternatively whether the ill-health conditions the attitudes (or conceivably vice versa). But it is clear that whereas the readiness to trust women and the capacity to be confident in dealings with them is much reduced following divorce, the level of sexual interest, which presumably derives from less cerebral instincts, is enhanced more often than it is diminished.

Attitudes to Remarriage

We asked the question: '*If you are not now remarried, how keen are you to marry again?*' Twenty-six of the ninety-two men had in fact remarried since their divorce so these were excluded from the analysis on the grounds that since they had done so they presumably had been keen to do so. We collected no systematic information on how these second marriages were working out. For the sixty-six men who had not remarried, opinion divided as follows on the idea of remarriage:

	Number of men
Very keen	8
Fairly keen	17
Indifferent	25
Fairly hostile	8
Never again	8
	66

Thus the number of men favourable to a new marriage heavily outnumbered those who were not, with the largest group of all remaining indifferent. Comments about remarriage ranged from those which indicated a clear need for security:

. . . [I am] less gregarious and more pessimistic and have a greater need to have a secure home and someone to share it.

to those who are not sure it would work:

. . . however much one rationalises and genuinely accommodates the loss, there is always a slight, hardly conscious, feeling of wishing not to 'fail' in the same way again.

One man had sorted the issues out in an enviably comprehensive fashion:

I have reconsidered totally the role of male/female relationships, understood (somewhat) existentialism—practically—gained immeasurable freedom to open up and practice ways of living, analysed nuclear families and their role under capital, realised *long-term*, exclusive, 'couple' relationships do not suit me.

When examining the pattern of answers in greater detail certain reasonably clear relationships emerged. Age seems to have some effect since the average age of those keen to remarry was 38 compared to 45 for those hostile to the idea—a considerable difference. It is equally clear that is would be wrong to envisage a swing from hostility to keenness as memories of the first failure receded. Surprisingly the evidence points to the reverse conclusion since the group most hostile to the idea of a second attempt had been divorced nearly five years; those most keen to try again had been divorced, on average, only about nineteen months. Possibly the longer-divorced men who were keen on remarriage have, in fact, remarried.

Another characteristic that marks out those keen to remarry is their generally more friendly attitude to their ex-wife; half of them still regard her in a friendly light whereas only one of the sixteen men hostile to remarriage continues to do so. But, slightly paradoxically, it is those most ready to blame her for what happened, or at least to be non-accepting of the necessity for a break-up, who are much the more ready to try again. It seems, typically, that readiness to remarry is associated with regret and non-acceptance that the first marriage ended but also with a noticeable lack of rancour towards the former partner. This may indicate that in the minds of some men the break-up was perhaps a matter of bad luck which could be reversed next time. This seems to reflect a very different frame of mind from the group who, on average five years later, are still very bitter towards their ex-wife and strongly opposed to remarriage. This latter group, incidentally, are also much less in touch with their former set of mutual friends.

One other circumstance surrounding the divorce seems to bear on the issue. The men who moved out from the matrimonial home, or were obliged to do so, are marginally against remarriage whereas those who stayed in the home are keen to remarry by a ratio of three to one. Some of the latter have custody of the children (one of the reasons for continuing occupancy) and might be expected to be interested in remarriage partly for this reason. Others are left surrounded by the 'hardware' of a shared life and a home carefully built up with a pair relationship in mind. No doubt the urge to share it (especially perhaps the domestic chores), plus the knowledge that one has a ready made home to offer, lead some men to seek a new partner all the more actively.

If post-divorce domestic arrangements seem to bear on the issue of remarriage so too does the extent to which career and finances have been affected. For example, of the men who feel that their careers suffered only temporary disruption, or even benefit, after the break-up, nearly three-quarters wish to remarry. By contrast, in the group reporting permanent career damage, the balance of feeling is against remarriage. The same tendency is even more strikingly evident in relation to financial ill-effects. Those who feel they lost out heavily the first time around are much more often against remarriage than are the rest. The final factor to be considered was mental health. Again an effect was evident; the men reporting new mental health problems subsequent to divorce were in favour of the idea of remarriage by nineteen to nine. Of those with no mental health problems the pros and the antis were evenly balanced.

The pattern of answers to the question about remarriage acquires a subtly different significance when studied in the light of the full range of post-divorce circumstances. There was an apparent association of 'keenness' to remarry with a range of essentially practical circumstances (such as whether still in an established home, how badly affected in terms of employment and finance) and this seems to indicate that many of the respondents might in fact have been giving an assessment of how well placed they were in practical terms to embark on remarriage rather than expressing degrees of preference for such a course in any abstract way. In other words the *desire* to remarry might, for many, be unconsciously conditioned by an assessment of their *capacity* to remarry in the light of domestic and financial circumstances. Certainly several of the men we interviewed, who had lost the use of their previous home and were heavily burdened with maintenance payments, led a social life which was closely limited by such practical considerations. Thus they could see many difficulties in the way of starting again and perhaps adding new responsibilities to the old. If this is true in a substantial number of cases it seems clear that financial and property settlements are significant not only in terms of winding up a former partnership; they may also have far-reaching implications for the man's capacity to develop a satisfactory new life-style and to embark on another marriage. We will return to this point in the final chapter.

Attitudes to the Divorce Laws

The last question on the form was designed to supplement the discussion on the specific feelings concerning solicitors (see Chapter

6) with an assessment of feeling on the overall experience of the legal process. We asked: '*Finally, do you feel that the present divorce laws, as you experienced them are . . .?*' to which there was a strongly marked pattern of results:

	Number of men	
Strongly in favour of women	54 ⎫	68
Rather in favour of women	14 ⎭	
Pretty fair	21	
Rather in favour of men	1 ⎫	1
Strongly in favour of men	0 ⎭	

Feeling on this issue ran extremely strong and the following was not the only comment to indicate a clear sense of alienation from the system at large:

It may sound silly, but I was a loyal citizen before the break-up. Now I wouldn't lift a finger on behalf of a country that has financed my financial destitution by a vicious vindictive woman.

It is worth noting that this general question about the state of the law came immediately after one asking for a judgment on the fairness or otherwise of the *actual financial arrangements* now in force between the respondent and his ex-wife. To this question the balance of answers was:

| Very fair or quite reasonable | 39 |
| Rather unreasonable or very unfair | 29 |

These apparently contradictory patterns of response, taken in combination, seem to show that many men in the sample had made a clear distinction between their particular case (judged to be quite fair) and the general situation (judged to be strongly in favour of women). Or possibly it was issues unconnected with finance, perhaps custody arrangements or the cost of legal services, that led so many to feel so strongly about sex bias in current divorce laws.

Because of the unequal way opinion was divided we sorted the responses into two groups; those who felt the law was fair or even favoured men (22 men) and those who felt it was biased in favour of women (68 men). Those who felt it was unfair tend also to feel far more often either that the break-up was primarily the fault of their ex-wife or, alternatively, that it was an unfortunate mistake. Those who, by contrast, feel it is even-handed also feel much less judgmental and more accepting about the way in which the marriage ended. Similarly it is the group who themselves petitioned, thus taking a decision and an initiative, who are less emphatic that the law favours women. Of the forty-five men who were petitioned by their ex-wives, only five see the law as 'pretty fair' and twenty-nine see it as strongly favouring women. Similarly those who still feel very hostile to their ex-wife judge, with only three exceptions, that the law favours women. By contrast the majority of those more friendly to their former partner judge the law to be even-handed or even to favour men.

We might expect that the degree of disruption to career and financial position would lead to strong feelings about sex bias in the law. This turned out to be correct in both respects. As the degree of both career and financial disruption increases so does the weight of opinion concerning adverse bias in the law. This is especially true in the large group who had suffered serious financial effects who judged by a ratio of six to one that the law favoured women. Finally, when considering the impact of mental health problems we found that a very marked feeling about sex bias in the law is evident amongst those who have experienced mental health difficulties since the divorce. Less than a fifth of this group see the law as fair whereas in the group free of such problems opinion was evenly divided.

It seems evident that the conclusions drawn by the men in the sample concerning the fairness of the law were overwhelmingly determined by aspects of their own case. This is not at all surprising, since divorce is for most a once in a lifetime event and few, if any, of those embarking on marriage (as we point out in our 'Afterthoughts') will have been encouraged to discuss possible lines of action if and when things go wrong. There is thus no chance to base opinions about the fairness of the legal system either on repeated personal experience or on rational prior discussion. But none of this really helps to explain why a clear majority of men felt the outcome of their own case was at least tolerably fair *financially* while at the same time holding such strong collective feelings about the way the law in general favours women.

How Angry Still?

In the previous chapter we discussed our respondents' assessments of the *effects* of their marriage break-up on four important areas of life; friendships, career, financial position and mental health. We combined these effects together for each man and identified a 'least affected' and a 'most affected' group. But we also decided it was important to assess the *feelings* our respondents had about what had happened and especially to look into the amount of anger that remained. 'Anger' is easier to feel and recognise than to define since it is so closely bound up with the related feelings of hurt, frustration, powerlessness and guilt. Nevertheless, what might loosely be termed anger seemed to be present in virtually all cases. Not only that, but differences in the strengh of angry feelings seemed to be a key factor in explaining many other differences in attitudes and behaviour. On these grounds and despite the obvious problem of putting a value on a very complex feeling, we judged it worthwhile to assess the differences in the levels of anger felt by the men in the sample, to try to determine the circumstances that might help to explain these differences, and especially to see whether the amount of anger seems to have lessened over time.

We therefore considered, for each man, his answers on the following issues (all of which have been discussed separately earlier in the book) because we felt that all of them, in different ways, revealed how strongly each man was feeling:
— feelings about why the break-up had occurred
— feelings about his ex-wife
— feelings about his ex-wife's new partner (if any)
— feelings about women in general
— assessments, positive or negative, about changes in himself
— opinions concerning the financial settlement in his case
— opinions about the state of matrimonial law in general.

As we saw earlier, reactions to each of these questions had varied a great deal in terms of the strength of feeling expressed. On each of the seven issues we had previously categorised the comments into one of five groups ranging from answers that gave a very friendly, accepting, rational or positive view (given a value of one) to those that gave an angry, hostile account (given a value of five). Answers somewhere in between were given values of two, three or four depending how they varied between the two extremes. These values from one to five were then simply added up for each man. The total score gave a fair indication of how angry each man was still feeling, with high scores reflecting high anger over the whole range of issues and low scores the reverse.

We then separated out the nineteen men with the *lowest* total score and the eighteen men with the *highest* total score and tried to see what it was, apart from differences in the level of anger still felt, that distinguished the two groups. Some very clear differences emerged as shown in the summary below.

	The least angry group	The most angry group
Type of employment	All except two in non-manual jobs	The majority in manual jobs
Who petitioned	Husbands and wives equally	Wives outnumbered husbands three to one
Children	Mostly childless	All except two have chilldren in ex-wife's custody
General relationships	Largely unaffected	Closer to parents, less close to friends
Mental health	Half had no such problems, most other had only minor problems	*All* had problems, nearly all of them developed since the divorce
Career and financial effects	Clear pattern of increasing anger as the effect increases—more marked for financial impact than for career impact	
Attitude to remarriage	*All* either keen or neutral about remarriage	Over half actively hostile to remarriage

When the group of fifty-five fathers with children in the mother's custody was considered it was found that, on average, those in contact with their children harboured considerably less anger than those who were not. Equally, the group who had remarried was on average less angry than those who had remained single. In fact the angriest group by far was those who had children in the ex-wife's custody, lived less than ten miles from them but did not see them, and had remained unmarried. This group, consistently, gave very hostile and angry answers to the various questions asked and it is clear that the feelings generated by the break-up are more likely to be reinforced and stimulated in these circumstances than when fathers either have contact with their children, or remarry, or move right away. We feel there are important conclusions to be drawn from this findings both for judicial policy and for individual negotiation about contact with children.

Our system for producing a 'score' of the strength of *feeling*, combined with our assessment in the last chapter of the *impact* of the break-up (in terms of friendships, career, finances and health) enabled us to compare these two assessments for each respondent. Given no variations in personality, a strong similarity could be expected between the two. In other words one would expect those who declared they had suffered the greatest damage to their lives to be the people who also felt most angry about events. In fact when we carried out this analysis this strong relationship was found. But there was also a group of men who had apparently suffered considerable impact and felt very little anger and conversely another group whose answers denoted far more anger than the reported facts seemed to warrant. Clearly this is because personalities *do* vary enormously, especially in terms of strength and resilience in the fact of adverse events. This seems to point the way for further research which might be directed towards identifying exactly what qualities, or break-up circumstances, enable people to cope with divorce without suffering high levels of destructive anger.

Our final analysis produced a thought-provoking result. The level of anger in each man's answers was compared with the number of years since his divorce. We did this because it seemed reasonable to believe that 'time heals all' and that, in general, feelings might have cooled over time. An unexpected answer emerged: *there was no relationship at all between the two values*. In other words there was no evidence whatsoever that long-divorced men felt any lower (or higher) degrees of anger than recently-divorced men. It is possible to attribute this curious findings to the way the research was done. We were not able to assess the changes of feeling *of each individual man* over time. We could only compare the assessed level of anger with the time since divorce for each man in the sample as a whole. It is also possible that the result stemmed wholly or in part from the sampling method we were obliged to use. Clearly those who feel moved to respond to an advertisement, and to complete a survey form, may well continue to feel more strongly about the issues than the general run of divorced men (although this would not necessarily mean that they feel more *angry* about them).

But we would not wish to see the finding entirely disregarded on the grounds of insecure methodology. It is possible that the anger stemming from a marriage failure concentrates into a hard knot of feeling that remains lodged in the mind. The external signs may be that the anger has gone away or at least receded since there is a limit to the extent to which it can be revealed unless one's contact with friends and acquaintances is to be placed at risk. But the submergence of the anger in a social or even mental sense may not, for many men, be the same as its total evaporation. Given an unexpected new outlet, such as that provided by the completion of a survey form, feelings of considerable strength may be (and were) revealed. We therefore regard it as an open question whether or not it is our research method that has produced the result that anger about the divorce does not appear to lessen significantly over time. We do, however, feel that the implications are so serious that some further research should be initiated to see whether our finding has substance. If it does, more thought must urgently be given to possible ways of helping individuals to cope with their anger sooner rather than later.

Chapter 9
The Way Forward

Many of the difficulties and strains experienced by divorcing men are highlighted in the courts where lawyers and judges interpret the present divorce laws to fit the particular circumstances of the case. The law is primarily concerned with balancing the rights of all the parties taking into account their past behaviour and assessing their likely future needs. We have already examined men's experiences of their solicitors, their views about the adversarial nature of the court proceedings, and their attitudes about the present law. Inevitably there will always be dissatisfaction in the legal outcomes since individuals are mainly concerned with their own definitions of rightness and fairness which do not necessarily coincide with judicial judgments. However the issue remains—how can necessary reforms be brought about? We discuss the major ways in which important changes are already taking place or are under discussion. Firstly, we examine the current state of the law especially as it relates to financial provision and review the various arguments for reform. Whilst we examine in detail the English and Scottish proposals for reform we are aware that the issues under review are pertinent to all other societies where divorce is available. Secondly, we discuss how services to help with post-divorce problems and adjustments can be better developed.

The Law—Arguments for Reform

In an interview given on divorce reform (*The Times*, 30 January 1980) Leo Abse, MP, a key parliamentary figure in promoting the changes which resulted in the 1969 Divorce Law Reform Act, said of the Act:

It was built on obsolescence . . . we were legislating on a staircase moving so rapidly that if I ever had any illusions that this was the last word on the subject they were rapidly shattered by the changing role of women. The big battle at the time was with those opponents of the Bill who claimed that it would licence the middle-aged men to abandon their wives and marry their secretaries.

The stringent financial safeguards for women included in the Act were put in to placate the lobby representing women who were fearful of being divorced against their wishes and left financially impoverished. Abse went on to comment that whilst the Act did away with the court contest between the warring parties to decide on innocence and guilt, 'the old conflicts have been transferred from battles about guilt to arguments over money, children and property.'

It has been argued that there is another anomaly in our divorce laws which results from the legal abolition of a search for fault and blame and its replacement with the principle of 'irretrievable breakdown'. Despite the establishment of this principle the majority of divorces still involve one party alleging wrong-doings of the other. As evidence of this 65 per cent of divorce petitions are filed on the grounds of 'unreasonable behaviour' or adultery; the two-year and five-year separation grounds are much less commonly used in practice.

Cases may be less often contested in open court as a result of the 1969 Act (only 1 or 2 per cent of cases are contested) but this means only that the conflicts have shifted into the private area, either between the parties directly or more often between solicitors. The law may have changed the principles and rules for deciding marital dissolution but its practice and implementation suggest that while the traditional adversarial system persists 'it will almost inevitably be the case that such litigation will serve as the focus for the partners' deep-seated feelings of rejection, hurt and distress' (English Law Commission, 1981). Nowhere in the system is the adversarial aspect clearer than over the division of property and financial settlements. Whilst the law has moved towards a 'no-guilt' basis for ending the marriage, judgments concerning the couple's financial rights and needs still involve the court in considering all the circumstances *including the conduct of the partners during the marriage*. It is the failure to integrate the criteria for terminating the marriage with the criteria for sorting out issues to do with money that lies at the heart of the present agitation for the reform of the divorce laws.

In response to growing disquiet about the working of the divorce laws in relation to financial provision, the Scottish and English Law Commissions have each produced a discussion paper containing a review of the policy and evolution of the existing law, an analysis of the main criticisms and a discussion of some alternative 'models' for arbitrating financial provision. As a result of the responses to and comments on these papers, and in the case of the Scottish one also of the findings of some sponsored research, further papers have been produced which contain recommendations for reform. We shall examine some of the key problems in the light of these various legal discussions.

MAINTENANCE AND PROPERTY

The Matrimonial Causes Act of 1973 which consolidated the previous legislation (the Divorce Law Reform Act 1969, the Law Reform (Miscellaneous Provisions) Act 1970 and the Matrimonial Proceedings and Property Act 1970) contained the provisions for dealing with all financial arrangements and gave the court wide powers in all areas of maintenance and property apportionment (see section 25 of the Act). In considering what provisions should be made the court should have regard to:

1. The income, earning capacity, property and other financial resources which each of the partners to the marriage has or is likely to have in the foreseeable future.
2. The financial needs, obligations and responsibilities which each of the partners to the marriage has or is likely to have in the foreseeable future.
3. The standard of living enjoyed by the family before the breakdown of the marriage.
4. The age of each party to the marriage and the duration of the marriage.
5. Any physical or mental disability of either of the partners to the marriage.
6. The contributions made by each of the partners to the welfare of the family, including any contributions made by looking after the home or caring for the children.

The Scottish Law Commission (1981) considered that such a list 'does not go far enough in the direction of principles and predictability. There is no acceptable way of specifying how much weight should be given to the various factors, some of which pull in opposite directions'. They concluded that the 'factors are so numerous and so various that discretion is likely in the end to be as wide as it would be without the list'. They favoured a system based on 'a combination of principles or objectives' because in their view this would better correspond 'to reality'. The system they proposed aimed 'to strike the right balance between principles and discretion'. They took the view that the present system 'leaves too much unfettered discretion to the court'.

The main source of the maintenance problem stems from Section

25(1) of the 1973 Matrimonial Causes Act which states that the courts are:

... directed to have regard to various factors and so to exercise their powers as to place the partners, so far as it is practicable, *and having regard to their conduct*, just to do so, in the financial position in which they would have been if the marriage had not broken down and each had properly discharged his or her financial obligations and responsibilities towards the other [emphasis added].

As an editorial in *The Times* argued (13 September 1980), 'that aim is clearly unattainable, and in some cases absurd. It is both an unrealistic objective for the majority of divorced people whose financial resources are insufficient to provide adequately for another, and it reinforces the concept of dependency after divorce. The marriage thus lives on even though the parties no longer live together'. As Deech wrote in *The Times* (14 February 1980), maintenance is:

... inimical to sexual equality and operates to the long-term detriment of women .... The concept of female dependence and the sexual stereotypes of husband as provider, wife as full-time housekeeper and mother still exist and serve to perpetuate the common law proprietary relationship of the husband and wife after dissolution of the marital bond .... While they express the superiority of the male, the maintenance laws are at the same time an irritant to the increasing number of divorced men (many believing themselves to be the 'innocent' party to the divorce) who suffer the perpetual drain on their income represented by a former wife, although the amount she actually receives is unlikely to be sufficient for her upkeep.

Some of the present dissatisfaction stems from the earlier history of divorce and the case law decisions since 1973. The wife's entitlement to alimony was established in the nineteenth century when divorce and the freedom to remarry were heavily restricted, (see Chapter 1). Divorce was possible only for the wealthy and usually the money lay in the hands of the husband. It was therefore relatively straightforward for the court to make such provision for the wife as would allow her to continue to live at her previous standard of living. The stereotype of the breadwinning male and the dependent female may have fitted the prevailing socio-economic and political structure at the time, but changes in the position, status, expectations and opportunities for women throughout the second half of this century have eroded many of the distinctions that previously existed between the economic position of husbands and wives.

Section 25 of the 1973 Act failed to specify the criteria for assessing individual cases of financial need, as is evidenced by its very general language. As a result the courts have been obliged to develop their own interpretations of this section. The broad formula now adopted by the courts as a result of a number of Court of Appeal rulings is to give the wife up to a half of the capital of the marriage, and one-third of the joint earnings, with something for each of the children which in many cases is about one-fifth. This formula has created considerable financial problems for all parties concerned and particularly the parties of any second or subsequent marriages. Although the law allows for flexibility in dealing with individual cases, in practice the general formula is now well established and in most cases is the sole criterion for calculating financial settlements. Its major weakness is that in many instances it is too rough and ready to deal with the changing needs of the parties and the resources available to meet them.

It has been argued that the present law on property and maintenance is adequate because it allows for flexibility and individual interpretation and that when one examines the practice of the law it 'can be seen to fall into a number of neat series of cases each turning on its own particular facts' (Rakusen, 1979). For instance there was a High Court case where both parties had remarried following the divorce; whereas the wife remarried a 'wealthy' man the husband had remarried an 'impecunious women'. In deciding to award the ex-wife a much smaller part of the assets than that sought, it was argued that the guiding principle of Section 25 of the 1973 Act refers to the parties of the marriage and it is not the wife alone who is to be placed in the same position as if the marriage had not broken down. Unfortunately there are many more cases where the circumstances are *not* as neat and clear-cut where, for example, only one party remarries or there are children of a second marriage to support. We therefore consider that the issues of property and maintenance remain at the very least untidy and serve often to perpetuate the marital difficulties long after the marriage has been declared 'dead'. Whilst the contradiction remains between a non-guilt-based divorce law and a practice for settling financial and property arrangements that *is* based on the conduct and behaviour of the parties whilst married, the emotional battles will continue to be fought out in pursuit of the irreconcilable principles of justice and equality.

An alternative proposal is that 'the primary aim of maintenance, when payable, should be rehabilitative, e.g. husband to support wife for three years only while she undergoes retraining or until the youngest child has started school. The case for permanent maintenance should be made only for the older women after a long marriage' (Deech, *The Times*, 14 February 1980). This suggestion is based on the view that marriage is no longer a secure area for life for a woman, and that 'her retreat into the home and motherhood during marriage ought to be treated as her own choice and not forced on her by her husband.' Women ought to have the right to be treated as 'capable of self-support'. A variation of this view (echoing Leninist edicts in post-revolutionary Russia) is that 'it would be logical to abolish maintenance altogether in time with the achievement of true equality for women, especially in employment. But that equality is still far away in practice, and to abolish maintenance to first wives would not conform with the reality of family and economic life today.' The problem of any legal reform is to reconcile the harsh economic realities facing many women with their right to be treated equally and independently.

SHOULD MARITAL CONDUCT MATTER?

Conduct refers to the behaviour of the partners to one another throughout the period of the marriage and the major legal question is how much, if at all, this behaviour before the divorce should be considered as relevant evidence in deciding financial settlements. The Scottish Law Commission (1981) devoted a considerable amount of discussion to this issue. Apart from the difficulty of weighing and assessing evidence to do with conduct and the probability that such a clause is 'calculated to increase animosity and bitterness', their view is that decisions over conduct and its relevance leave too much room for interpretation by individual judges. They considered that such a clause was 'an abdication of responsibility by Parliament in favour of the judiciary'. However they recognised that if conduct and behaviour were ignored altogether it 'would lead to results which members of the public would find unacceptable'. Nevertheless, they were aware of the contradiction in the present law: 'It is inconsistent with the no-fault philosophy of the present divorce law to make matrimonial misconduct a significant factor in the assessment of financial provision'. In arriving at their recommendation regarding the relevance of behaviour and conduct they recognised the many difficulties of administering the present all-embracing reference to past conduct and suggest 'that courts of law are not necessarily well equipped to decide such questions', that 'it would be surprising if all judges had the same views on questions of marital conduct', and that 'the present "rule" does nothing to encourage an amicable settlement'. Their proposal is that:

. . . the conduct of the parties, except where it has affected the basis of the claim for financial provision, should be taken into account only in relation to the principles of fair provision, adjustment to independence and relief of grave financial hardship, and then only if it would be manifestly inequitable to leave that conduct out of account.

By contrast, the English Law Commission (1981) made no new proposals with regard to conduct as a factor in fixing maintenance. The analysis of the evidence it had received showed a 'considerable body of conflicting comment'. On one hand, some individuals 'felt a considerable sense of injustice because the court had not been prepared to take account of the other spouse's behaviour in assessing financial provision'. But on the other hand, the Commission accepted that it would be very time-consuming and expensive for courts to examine each case in terms of apportioning blame for the breakdown of the marriage. Moreover such an exercise could never be very precise due to the lack of tools '. . . for dissecting the complex inter-actions which go on all the time in a family' (Justice Ormrod, 1973). Furthermore the Commission argued against any system which was likely to foster mutual recriminations. It favoured a system which 'encourages the parties to come to terms with their often deep-seated feelings of resentment and anger and which would be helpful in encouraging them to come to terms with their new situation'.

The Commission therefore recommended no change in the present wording of Section 25 of the 1973 Matrimonial Causes Act with its reference to conduct as a factor which courts can consider in making financial provision. It considered that the freedom for judges to decide when conduct is a relevant issue allows greater flexibility in interpreting the law to fit individual circumstances. With the increasing number of rulings by the Court of Appeal there are sufficient guidelines to assist all courts in deciding when to exercise the conduct criterion. The Commission's overall view was that judges are now better able to 'get a feel of the case' where an examination of conduct is relevant.

The main danger of the present law, as the Scottish Law Commission argued, may well be that it gives too much discretion to judges to decide when the examination of conduct is relevant or not. The English Law Commission hoped that with the general shift in emphasis towards encouraging economic independence after divorce, and with the hoped for growth in the number of conciliation schemes attached to courts, there would be less need for courts to assess the relevance of conduct. It could however be argued that whilst the criterion of conduct remains available to litigants there will always be cases coming to the courts for adjudication which will result in more Court of Appeal rulings. This in turn will affect the financial settlements made in the lower courts. Moreover, so long as the responsibility for exercising discretion lies with the judges, there will be little predictability and certainly for the litigants as to how the court might interpret the conduct clause.

THE POSITION OF SECOND WIVES

Another problem which has provoked considerable disquiet concerns the financial position of second wives in relation to the husband's first family. The court is not obliged to consider the needs of the second marriage when making provision for the first wife and children. Yet the second wife's capital and income may be taken into account when the court makes the financial settlement. We thus have a state of affairs whereby it is possible to obtain a no-fault divorce, where the man is free to remarry and yet, if he does, *the second wife's economic needs are ignored*. However, if she has an income and any assets these will be considered as part of the total resources when fixing the financial settlement for the *first* wife and family. Naturally enough this anomaly is at the centre of the current debate for reform as it produces strong resentment.

In an article in *The Times* (16 January 1980) on the position of second wives Drummond has shown that 'second wives tended not to object to their husbands support of first wives, not even to an increasing contribution over the years. What they object to vehemently was their own earnings and capital being included as part of their husband's income when maintenance to a previous wife was assessed.' 'I have been supporting my children for years', wrote one second wife, 'now her's take preference over mine.' Perhaps not surprisingly, given the embattled and emotionally charged nature of the problems, feelings run high amongst all parties. Some first wives maintained that they had an entitlement to the second wife's money as a right as well as to their second husband's. With equal righteousness one remarried ex-husband wrote,

the second time around marriage bond, especially when the bridegroom was the plaintiff in a divorce case, is nothing more than a charter for parasites. It gives total freedom to the first wife to bleed her ex-husband emotionally and financially . . . frankly somebody be it clergy or registrar, should be bound by law to spell out exactly what lies in store for the would-be second wife.

Such comments indicate the strength of feelings about the present state of the law. But there remains the simple problem, as identified by Berlins, that 'there is not enough to go round' (*The Times*, 3 September 1980). He doubts whether 'any system of law can make a limited income satisfy the needs of two families. Someone has to suffer, but the courts usually try to ensure that it is not the first wife. It is impossible to do justice to both first and second families.' The problems posed by courts as a result of favouring the first family at the expense of the second are considerable, particularly for the second wife and her new relationship. As Drummond (1981) found in her study of second wives,

Second wives describe their predecessors as living in comfort in the home of the first marriage while the new family faces a miserable existence in inadequate accommodation. Many have to go out to work to supplement the new husband's stretched income while the ex-wife, although capable of working, can sit back and accept the monthly maintenance cheque.

One married man we interviewed showed how he pays over 70 per cent of his income to his ex-wife; she is not working, even though the children are at school, and she continues to live in the matrimonial home with all the facilities and conveniences built up during the marriage. Meantime he struggles to survive in humbly furnished small accommodation with a substantial subsidy from his new partner, who also has a child, and her family. The struggle to make ends meet financially is a major source of friction between the new couple and threatens their relationship. Their bitterly felt concern is that even when the children have grown up they will continue to be obliged to support his first wife until she either dies or remarries.

The Scottish Law Commission's approach to the financial position of second wives was to consider them in terms of third parties in general, and in this way they concluded, 'the resources of an employer, brother or co-habitee would, as such, be extraneous and irrelevant factors' in the assessment of maintenance'. However in phrasing their recommendations they recognised that 'any economic advantages derived by either party to the divorce from third parties, should, in our view be regarded as part of the circumstances of the case, or, where appropriate, as affecting that party's resources, even if they are unenforceable.' In other words, the court would consider the second wife's income and assets only in the wider context of the overall assessment of the needs and resources of all the parties involved.

By contrast, the English Law Commission (1981) did not make any recommendations to ease the 'intractable problem' of the extent to which a second wife's means and resources should be taken into account. Whilst appreciating the resentment felt and expressed by second wives and by men who had remarried, and the damage often inflicted on second marriages, the Commission took a very strict line for maintaining the present procedures which allow the courts to consider the second wife's resources in the assessment of maintenance:

Nevertheless it seems to us to be not only logical but just that, if the Order in favour of the first wife (and her children) is of an appropriate amount, the husband should not be allowed to escape from that obligation by pleading that he needs to keep all his income for the necessary support of his second family, when this is not in fact the case. What would be involved in abandoning the present practice would often be a transfer of the husband's proper obligation in respect of his first wife to the State.

Clearly the Commission tended towards the view that it is 'proper' to regard the contract of marriage, even if it is subsequently terminated, as a life-long financial commitment. Consequently they did not consider it appropriate to recommend any changes in the present law.

However, having asserted very sharply the moral right of the first family to have first call on the combined resources of the second marriage, the Commission hoped that some of their other proposals, if carried out, would result in less injustice and feelings of resentment. These included:

(i) fixing an appropriate level of support for the first wife;
(ii) giving greater emphasis to the first wife's earning potential and to the desirability of securing a smooth transition to independence in appropriate cases.

If the English Law Commission's view does prevail it will certainly confirm and reinforce the inferior status of second marriages. However the net effect of such proposals would be to increase strains on these marriages and ultimately oblige the 'State', through supplementary benefits, to give financial support to a proportion of them. Moreover the assertion of the primacy of the first family's needs over the second in such unequivocal terms is likely to exacerbate feelings of resentment, bitterness and injustice in all the parties involved, which in turn is likely to affect, as we have seen in our study, the extent and quality of contact between fathers and their children.

Another related theme was taken up by a spokesman for the Campaign for Justice in Divorce who wrote about the issue of maintenance once the children are independent.

Does either party to a broken marriage have a life-long (and even post-mortem) financial claim on the other when that person fails to marry? If society accepts that such a liability is no longer valid in view of the social changes that have occurred, particularly the increasing popularity (and vulnerability) of second marriages—themselves an attempt at social repair—then, if an ex-wife is prevented from working by incapacity or the lack of available employment or if she simply chooses not to work, she will not be the liability of her former husband, but would have to be deal with in the same way as any other citizen in these circumstances (*The Times*, 22 September 1981).

The unending payments to the former spouse until either death or remarriage, and the uncertainty about the calculations, clearly increase the stress and strain on second marriages and leave a large loophole for the unscrupulous ex-wives to 'take their ex-husbands to the cleaners'. There is a counter argument to any contractual formula to protect the rights of second and subsequent spouses. This is quite simply that no formula could be devised which could be applied without modification to any circumstance and this would therefore mean continued reliance on the judge's discretion in individual cases. It would also make life difficult for those who had married on the basis of quite different expectations. We see all these difficulties as powerful reinforcement for the arguments we advance in our 'Afterthoughts'.

ALTERNATIVE BASES OF ARBITRATION

The Scottish Law Commission discussed a number of alternative bases for 'models' for arbitrating the financial issues which we have already outlined. They range from the existing legal system under the 1973 Matrimonial Causes Act through to a prescribed mathematical approach whereby divorcing spouses' financial rights and obligations would be fixed by reference to a statutory formula which could be departed from, if need be, to take account of certain specified factors. Whilst each of these models has certain merits and would solve certain of the present problems, the main argument against each is that they fail to combine the elements of need and rehabilitation with the 'clean-break' approach to divorce. If legal divorce is intended to sever the marital relationship and allow each party to start afresh and rehabilitate himself or herself as is strongly recommended by the Scottish Law Commission then the law governing financial settlements ought to reflect the clean-break principle. In arguing for their proposals the Commission was concerned to devise principles which could be adapted to fit cases of special need where the clean-break approach might cause grave hardship. Throughout the report the emphasis is on promoting financial independence of the parties and discouraging prolonged dependence of one party on another. References to past conduct should be kept to a minimum and consideration of the second wife's income should be only one of the factors taken into consideration when making financial judgments. In keeping with the spirit of their proposals the Commission favoured a maximum period of three years from the date of divorce for financial support by the husband to his ex-wife. The purpose of the three-year period would be to provide sufficient time for adjustment to financial independence and adaptation to the marital breakdown. Financial support for any children of the marriage would continue as at present.

The Scottish report shows, in our view, a good appreciation of the social and economic realities facing divorcees. In recommending that three years should be the maximum period to adjust to economic independence it firmly rejected the premise behind the English law that a spouse has a lifelong right to maintenance after divorce (although in our view it may be optimistic to assume that divorced women can 'adjust' in three years in today's economic conditions). Sensibly, the report acknowledged that changing the law on financial provision for divorcees would not lead to a general improvement in the condition of one-parent families. To achieve these improvements would involve changes in employment opportunities and social facilities, all of which lay outside their realm of influence. While conceding these limitations the Scottish Commission did not see that they were arguments to be used against reform of the present system with its manifest limitations.

The Times, in an editorial on the Report (7 October 1981), agreed that the principle of a 'meal ticket for life' should be ended but considered the three-year rehabilitative period to be unjust because, firstly, it was 'too short a period for those divorces which leave a wife with very young children who need constant care for four or five years more', and secondly, it was not 'fair play' for the wife who had irretrievably diminished her own career and expectation for the sake of 'staying at home caring for children or even just devoting herself to supporting her husband's career'. The editorial conceded the argument for limited maintenance but would have preferred a scheme with more flexibility and cited schemes for assessing redundancy payments, which take into account length of service, as a possible analogy. It argued that '. . . the length of a marriage is a most important factor'. *The Times* pointed out, as had a previously quoted correspondent, that any alteration of the present system on the lines the Scottish Law Commission suggested would not redress the unequal position of women in the labour and employment market. For such a change to take place larger-scale legal and economic changes would need to occur. It was concluded that:

Until more genuine equality of opportunity is achieved, and a recession works against that aim, there cannot be genuine sharing of child care. Women will continue to have to take the primary responsibility, most of them do so willingly and happily: when things go wrong the law should err, if it errs at all, on their side.

The Scottish Commission's report has tackled most of the major contentious issues and made concrete recommendations which would, if implemented in England and elsewhere, at the very least address some of the ambiguities of the present system. The stress placed on clarifying the objectives of the law, and laying down principles to be applied with regard to each of the issues, would allow for much more predictability and uniformity. In general the Scottish Commission favoured a system of post-divorce settlements which recognised that divorce meant the end of a marriage and all that such an ending entailed. It argued that the main aim of the law and the courts is to enable the termination to take place tidily and fairly with the minimum possible anger and recrimination.

By contrast, the English Law Commission's Report (1981) stopped short of the more radical reforms recommended by its Scottish counterpart. Amongst its seven recommendations, number five is the most important as it refers to the celebrated Section 25 of the 1973 Matrimonial Causes Act which the Commission recommends should be amended in the following respects:

To seek to place the parties in the financial position in which they would have been had the marriage not broken down should no longer be the statutory objectives;

and:

. . . the guidelines contained in Section 25(i) of the Matrimonial Causes Act 1973 should be reviewed, to give greater emphasis to the following matters:
a) the provision of adequate financial support for children should be an overriding priority. (Administrative steps should also be taken to ensure that the courts have adequate and reliable information about the current cost of maintaining children);
b) the importance of each party doing everything possible to become self-sufficient should be formulated in terms of a positive principle: and weight should be given to the view that, in appropriate cases, periodical financial provision should be primarily concerned to secure a smooth transition from the status of marriage to the status of independence.

Unlike the Scottish Commission which recommended, with certain exceptions, a three-year cut-off for maintenance, the English Commission did not specify a 'target time' for the transition from marriage to independence. Although it favoured the general principles of a clean break and financial finality, it envisaged cases where it would continue to be appropriate to order one spouse to maintain the other indefinitely. Without a fixed time limit built into any new legislation, the courts would continue to exercise their discretionary power over the general principle of transitional maintenance. Much would depend on the tightness of the wording of any guidelines as to how long a transitional period might be. The first reaction from the Campaign for Justice in Divorce was one of disappointment, since they felt that the report merely represented a retreat from the present principle of trying to put the parties in the position they were in before their divorce.

We have already discussed the English Commission's views with regard to the controversial issues of the second wife's means and resources and the question of how far conduct should be taken into account when making financial provisions. It felt that there should be no changes in the law. The Commission saw no solution to such intractable problems but hoped that if certain other proposals were carried out there would be less injustice. Amongst these were recommendations which related to: (i) increasing the availability and scope of conciliation schemes and similar services, 'everything possible should be done to encourage recourse to conciliation rather than litigation'; (ii) reviewing and reforming the procedures of the courts handling matrimonial cases; and (iii) monitoring, through periodical reports to Parliament, the financial consequences of divorce.

It is clear that one of the main concerns of the English Commission was to uphold the moral and financial duties and responsibilities of the husband to his first wife and family at the cost of the second (or any subsequent) wife and family. One commentator saw this as a reflection of the Commission's wish to avoid more dependent ex-wives becoming a burden on Social Security and other State schemes. Whatever else one may think of the Commission's unequivocal assertion of the first husband's primary responsibility, it does at least indicate that they hold firmly to the view of marriage characterised in the first chapter of this book. As seen by the Commission, marriage is a lifelong relationship which, even if ended, still entails one party supporting the other for life. In contemporary society, and in view of all the contrary opinion we set out in Chapter 2, is this really appropriate? Or has marriage become (or become again) a more negotiable contract to be freely entered into and just as freely terminated with, where possible, no long-term economic interdependence between the parties? It should be said that the English Commission did at least recognise the dilemma. The problem for legislators is that society itself seems to be in a state of transition from a belief that the law *should* enforce lifelong rights, duties and responsibilities in marriage to a view which gives greater weight to the emotional elements of personal happiness and fulfilment. To illustrate its appreciation of the changing currents of opinion the Commission in its 1981 report compared two views of marriage and divorce: firstly Lord Cecil, in 1937, during the debate on the Matrimonial Causes Act said:

. . . the only argument for more divorce really is the hardship of indissoluble marriage, but this is not argument for it assumes a right of happiness. There is no such right. . . . The path of virtue may often lead to unspeakable misery. . . . The Christian must endure as his Lord endured.

By contrast the Commission doubts whether there would yet be general acceptance of an alternative view of marriage which would see it as no more than:

. . . some sort of relationship between two individuals of indeterminate duration, involving some kind of sexual conduct, entailing vague mutual property and support obligations, that may be formed by consent of both parties and dissolved at the will of either.

We would agree entirely. But as we argue in our 'Afterthoughts' there is much room for creative thinking about the institution of marriage in the enormous area between these two extreme positions.

The lack of consensus about the nature of marriage itself raises major doubts about whether changes in the arbitration of financial settlements can effectively improve the financial position of those who divorce and remarry. Whichever direction the law takes it would seem that any benefit for some will be at a cost to others. Neither of the two Law Commissions was optimistic about the effects of their recommendations but the Scottish Commission, in our view, is more in touch with changing social realities. Their arguments and conclusions do at least acknowledge that we live in a society which tolerates a wide range of views on moral issues and in which there is no uniform view about marriage.

Non-legislative Ways Forward

Whatever changes may occur in the law, it is evident that better facilities are needed to enable the parties involved in a divorce to settle their disputes as harmoniously as may be possible outside the courts. Such settlements save enormous amounts of public and private money in the form of court time, legal aid and legal fees. It is also clear from our research that in a substantial proportion of cases the adversarial spirit shown by lawyers has served to make it less, rather than more, likely that a spirit of friendship and co-operation will survive the divorce. Yet our research has shown how vitally important it is that these feelings should remain, especially if there are children of the marriage. One man, feeling anything but friendly, reached this conclusion:

Lawyers are quite the worst people to help settle divorce disputes. Whoever does take the job on they shouldn't be making money out of it.

We have much support for this view but would distinguish between issues of property and finance, where we can see no alternative to careful legal arbitration, and child custody issues, where the present system seems often insensitive and based on outdated assumptions. Some hard thinking therefore has to be done, especially on devising the means by which more varied, imaginative and above all conciliatory arrangements can be arrived at.

We do, in fact, find it both surprising and alarming that so little has been achieved in the field of conciliation. The failure to establish conciliation services or schemes is in part a consequence of the poor co-ordination of the many agencies involved. It also, however, reflects the confusion and ambiguity that exist about helping people to divorce. The values and priorities of the Social Services, the Probation Service, the Courts, and the Marriage Guidance Council are shaped by the moral and political climate. The setting up of specific services to help people divorce runs up against views about the sanctity of marriage and the family. We therefore have a situation where divorce is fairly easily obtainable but little or no help is given to cope with the massive quantity of financial and emotional distress that has resulted. Clearly no matter how much help is at hand there are unavoidable costs and there will always be casualties. However, there is good evidence that where conciliation and advisory services are available the costs and casualities can be significantly reduced.

A pioneer scheme in this country, the Bristol Courts Family Conciliation Service, which despite its name works independently of the Court, sets out to provide an opportunity in a neutral informal and non-judgmental setting, for separating and divorcing couples to explore the possibilities of reaching agreements over matters that would in all probability otherwise end up being contested in court. The Service aims to see clients at an early stage, often before the filing of a petition, and before the conflicts become chronic and positions entrenched. The work of the Bristol group and others in the United States suggests that in a large number of cases it is possible to replace the inherently stressful competitive and acrimonious Court litigation with a low stress, impartial, co-operative approach. In the words of Coogler, who has developed a conciliation service in America under the auspices of the Family Mediation Service:

Post divorce adjustment is facilitated by supporting individual responsibility; reducing conflicts between spouses, modelling co-operative conflict resolution and effecting a settlement both parties can live with. In so doing, the high percentage of settlements that are typically in default should be greatly reduced (Coogler, Webber and McHenry, 1979).

The spread of such services is a matter of political will; the case for them seems irrefutable and on the basis of our evidence we support it whole-heartedly.

CO-ORDINATION AND CO-OPERATION

Despite the frequent claims by politicians that they represent 'the party of the family there exists no coherent government family policy. Many official reports, including that of the Finer Committee (1974), have called for better co-ordination of family services and some have drawn attention to the high costs resulting from the present fragmentation in provision. Nowhere is this lack of co-ordination more apparent than in the field of marriage counselling, and the handling of divorce. There is no statutory service to which people can turn for advice on matrimonial matters. It is true that a wide range of statutory, voluntary and private agencies exists in relation to children, health, the law, housing, etc. There are also many self-help groups of divorced and separated people. But as we found in our survey very few men, despite the severity of their problems, actually make contact with any of these agencies.

One answer might be better co-operation of the available help, better co-ordination between local services and above all more publicity. More information on legal rights and local sources of help should be available from key locations that men are likely to attend such as doctors' surgeries, solicitors' offices, Department of Health and Social Security offices and Jobcentres. Perhaps a more active and sensitive role might also be played by local social service departments since it was strikingly evident from our survey findings (Chapter 5) that men involved in divorce are not, on the whole, much helped by social workers. Greater co-operation is also required at national level in order to ensure that the various policies arrived at by departments of state are more effectively co-ordinated. Such co-operation, which was called for in *Marriage Matters* (Working Party, 1979) would help to ensure that the expertise concerning family problems which has been accumulated by staff in a wide range of departments is more effectively shared. Co-operation at the national level might also serve as an example to encourage local agencies to work more effectively together.

The present trend, however, seems to be for individual agencies or groups to set up special projects to deal with specific aspects of the divorcee's problem. For example, Families Need Fathers and the Campaign for Justice in Divorce put a great deal of effort into helping divorced men contest custody and overcome access problems. Although these groups were extremely valuable in the limited number of cases in which they were used, our survey has shown clearly that divorced men experience a fairly predictable but complex *cluster* of interrelated problems as they struggle to cope with various kinds of loss. The scale and complexity of the problems may be too much for small voluntary agencies, however dedicated, to handle. Social isolation is one of these problems. This can be partly overcome by contact with individuals with similar experiences. At present the only groups that specifically address themselves to facilitating this contact are Divorced and Separated Clubs. These clubs are commonly seen as simply a place to meet new partners but their aims as expressed by the National Federation of Clubs for the Divorced and Separated include the changing of social attitudes 'to remove the pariah of divorce', reform of the legal system and the provision of representation for the interests of divorced and separated people.

All these groups are clearly worthwhile and provide much needed support in a number of cases. But the activity is small scale (in relation to the growing size of the problem), voluntary and unco-ordinated. Possibly a properly funded agency, with the aim of helping divorced people cope with their problems *in the round*, and with more political 'weight', might be a better way forward than the spontaneous proliferation of small ad hoc groups. In suggesting this we are, however, aware of the strong feelings endemic in this field and the wide differences in philosophy among the various groups that have come into existence.

Although better co-ordination and publicity for existing services would help, there remains the problem of encouraging men to seek assistance outside their network of family and friends when the sort of help required goes beyond that which the network can give. The conventional answer is to make the services better known so that more people will contact them. No doubt there are sound reasons, such as respect for privacy, why the individual is normally expected to come to the services rather than vice versa. However there are also reasons why this approach may not be effective in providing support and advice for divorcees. For many men the stigma of being divorced produces a reluctance to talk openly about the problems. Stigma is no doubt also an issue for many divorced women but those with younger children to care for necessarily come into contact with various health, welfare and education agencies where they are likely to meet others with similar difficulties and needs. Moreover the advertising material for single parents displayed in surgeries, libraries, and similar community centres is usually, to judge from the wording, prepared very much with women in mind.

For men, who may have lost the day-to-day contact with both partner and children, and who may be living in the kind of accommodation that is not well suited to entertaining, the world can rapidly become a very lonely place. Given that most men have been socialised since infancy not to talk freely about personal feelings, even to close friends, the emotional isolation can become almost complete. This isolation can help to fuel the worse feelings men have about themselves. In fact these feelings can develop into what might be called a 'self-fulfilling stigma reinforcing cycle'. The cycle starts with, for example, the man feeling 'guilty' about the break-up and about the 'damage', real or imagined, it may be causing the children. He therefore judges himself to be 'bad' and asssumes that others will judge him similarly. This feeling is reinforced by a selective reception of 'signals' from the world at large, and especially perhaps from social service agencies who for statutory and other reasons are geared to help mothers and children rather than lone males. These signals serve to confirm, and reinforce, this original assessment of himself. In fact he feels even worse and less able to engage in new encounters so that the downward spiral continues. Breaking out of this self-perpetuating stigmatising cycle is a major task to be tackled if progress is to be made and it probably depends, in most cases, on encountering others in a new, positive and constructive way.

USING THE WORKPLACE

Possibly one way out of this cycle would be to concentrate more effort on the place where the majority of men most frequently meet, where they most naturally give and receive support and where they are most fully accepted by others—at work. We were particularly struck by the extent to which men in the sample had approached workmates, colleagues and employers to discuss their problems and how helpful they had been. In various interviews we heard references to 'those at work who had similar problems' and it was obvious that much benefit has been derived from discussion with them. By contrast many men were reluctant to consider talking to 'strangers', 'outsiders' or people they did not know. Doctors and solicitors were alright because '. . . they know about these things and besides it's their job'.

The key to understanding the importance of the workplace may lie in the idea of identity and self-worth. The gap to be bridged between even a severe need and actually seeking help from unfamiliar sources seemed vast. We found that many men would rather 'hold on' to their problems if to do otherwise would risk their losing more self-esteem, being judged by others as a failure and generally feeling further undermined in their identity as men. We realised that many had defined themselves as men partly in their key roles as husbands and fathers. In a sense they had controlled their lives and the lives of others in the accepted male fashion. The end of the marriage, sought more often than not by the woman, ended all that. Nothing further could be risked. The only 'safe' place left to discuss the problems and to reveal the extent of the damage was, for a significant number, the workplace. Here colleagues and employers valued them on grounds *different* from those which had been undermined.

It might well be possible to built on this by developing support services for divorced men at their place of work. Such work-based schemes might aim:

  (i) to provide and publicise information about the availability of local advisory services and groups and encourage men to use them;
 (ii) to provide and distribute material on some of the more commonly experienced effects of divorce;
(iii) to provide, if possible, opportunities for men to talk about their difficulties so as to increase the awareness that the problems they are experiencing are, in fact, also being faced by thousands of others.
 (iv) to provide (perhaps via the company accountant) some taxation advice; at a time when every penny counts, many men do not have access to proper advice on their changed tax position and end up failing to claim proper allowance on maintenance payments or incurring an unnecessary tax liability on property transfers (Wylie, 1981/82).

Existing personnel and welfare departments, trade unions, professional organisations, clubs and other organistions where men meet to relax could all be valuable means by which such schemes could be implemented. In these familiar contexts it might be possible to encourage more men to accept that it is healthy and appropriate to seek help. Such a referral system, therefore, might be more effective than self-referral to an unfamiliar agency that may *appear* to be women-oriented.

We are aware from the research that a minority of employers actually discriminate against divorced men when it comes to career advancement. We naturally hope that these attitudes will change. We consider that for many employers there may be positive benefits to be derived from the course we suggest. We are aware that many divorced men are just about surviving in terms of their health and ability to do a good job of work. In fact nearly a quarter of the men in our sample judged that their capacity to do so had been permanently damaged. No one has yet assessed the resultant cost to employers of this incapacity to work properly, but it must be enormous. The provision of useful practical information, and an open environment in which to talk, might repair some of this damage and free some of the energy currently devoted to survival. Capacity to work effectively would be bound to benefit and for this reason, if for no other, we feel it would make sense for employers to consider developing schemes along the lines we propose.

Afterthoughts—Marriage in a Changing Society

Cultural patterns are not simply products of their time; they incorporate surviving aspects of all previous cultural patterns. They are made up of traditions of thought, values and institutions which regulate, for example, the relationships between people and other people, people and property, and people and god. These traditions and institutions, and the societal values they purport to enshrine, tend to survive or die out depending on changes in political thought and developments in scientific and technological knowledge. For example, some institutions (such as serfdom) have died out in our culture—at a certain point, while continuing to serve certain interests, they became politically unacceptable. Other institutions (perhaps the House of Lords) survive, but in forms widely regarded as outdated. In such forms they encompass elements which are clearly reflections of some previous cultural state. These elements survive either because they are so deeply rooted that change is extremely difficult to achieve or else because they suit the needs of identifiable powerful groups. In practice these two explanations are much the same thing; the outdated elements have often been consciously singled out for survival by politically powerful groups whose interests they serve. In such circumstances a major 'change point' occurs only when some traumatic upheaval reveals that society's tolerance is stretched to the limit. At this point the evidence of widespread demand for change becomes undeniable. The economic cost of preserving the outdated form may become unacceptable or a 'legitimation crisis' (Habermas, 1976) may lead many people to question the whole system in a politically dangerous way. Even then, if the forces of reaction are especially strong, the reform may well be hesitant, largely cosmetic or based on a limited appreciation of the problem.

The institution of marriage forms a deeply rooted part of most cultures past and present. But when seeking to understand its particular characteristics in our own society (for example, the expectation of lifelong monogamy, the economic dependence of the wife and the role expectations both during marriage and after a divorce) the analysis in the previous paragraph can be applied at almost every point.

Church marriage is a uniquely all-embracing institution in that it aims to regulate all three forms of relationship noted; that is, relationships between pairs of people (and between each of them and all other people), between them and their property, and between them and the deity. In this intention alone, in a period of minority church membership, declining deference to authority and accelerating rates of scientific and technological understanding, Christian doctrine on marriage has increasingly been called into question. The revolution in the mode of industrial production has profoundly affected social relations generally and has required a mobility of labour that has largely broken down the social controls previously exerted by the pattern of locally based three-generation families (grandparents, parents, children). Two major wars, based on weaponry that has killed millions of combatants and inevitably drawn the civil population into the action, have fundamentally changed the economic and political power of women. Much has been done to ease their access to higher education. The recent shift of labour from manufacturing to service activities has opened up for them vast new fields of employment opportunity. In the face of these technological and social developments, codes of matrimony based on patriarchy and female dependence, and which insist on strict lifelong monogamy, look distinctly archaic.

Have these archaic elements been singled out for survival by identifiable dominant groups whose interests they serve? Without resorting to too much conspiracy theory it is plausible to argue that they have. Early campaigners for the rights of women, notably in the 1790s Mary Wollstonecraft (who first characterised marriage as 'legalised prostitution') and the Owenites in the 1820s and 1830s (who wished to remodel marriage in their communities), have met with outraged hostility by clerics and politicians. This was largely because they called into question the appropriateness of lifelong monogamy and the subordinate status of women within it. This was seen as tantamount to supporting the worst Jacobin excesses of the French Revolution (see Tomalin, 1974 and Taylor, forthcoming 1983). In other words to threaten marriage was to threaten the established male-dominated religious, political and economic order. Dominant political groups then and now naturally seek to maintain good order and, equally naturally, dominant economic interests favour any arrangement that helps to ensure that women remain available as cheap labour whether at work or in the home.

In certain periods these tendencies to 'use' marriage to achieve specific political and economic ends became dramatically more visible and more closely associated with state power. This has been especially evident in totalitarian and fascist régimes. In Nazi Germany, for example, marriage became '. . . the biologically rooted institution for the preservation of racial purity . . .' (Reich, 1975). In somewhat less oppressive political systems such as our own the use of conventional marriage to under-pin the system proceeds less obviously but no less surely; little discussion of alternative approaches to marriage relations is encouraged as part of the formal educational curriculum, whilst the massive extension of owner occupation in twentieth-century Britain has linked the formalised pair relationship to property ownership (albeit debt-laden) in a way that is difficult and expensive to untangle. The 'conservative' interests are easy to identify. On almost all occasions when there has been conflict about the nature of marriage between forces for radical change and forces for reaction, the Christian church (inspired by Pauline teaching on sexuality and strong notions of patriarchy) has lined up in favour of reaction. With equal reliability the legal profession has been well content to play its specialist and lucrative part in sorting out the complexities of restrictive legal codes of marriage and divorce.

Has some traumatic upheaval revealed that society's tolerance is stretched to the limit? Clearly several developments have coalesced in the wake of the two world wars. By the mid-1960s the church/legal system was beginning to grind out some overdue reform of what had been widely recognised to be a very illiberal divorce code. The women's movement grew dramatically and women gained much better access to the rapidly expanding higher education sector. Perhaps the most significant change was scientific: the growth in availability of effective means by which women can control their own fertility and thus gain the potential for an historically unprecedented degree of sexual freedom and self-expression. It is crucially significant that the mass march away from marriage since the late 1960s, also historically unprecedented, has been led by women.

This march forms part of the evidence for a widespread demand for change—a backlash against centuries of church- and state-inspired patriarchy. We see much of the contents of this book as further evidence. The apparent viciousness of much of the behaviour, the bewilderment, damage and ill-health that has resulted in many lives, the fracturing of many parent/child relationships and the corresponding damage (which we have not been able to assess) to the lives of many of the women involved are themselves indicators of the extent to which the attitudes, legal codes and 'welfare' arrangements currently in use are hopelessly outdated and in-adequate. People are caught up in a web of confused religious dogma, archaic legal thought and practice, and consequent muddled expectations about how they should behave in marriage. The effects are beginning to look positively inhumane and certainly costly. Lord Cecil's injunction (see Chapter 9) that the Christian should be prepared to endure 'unspeakable misery' in marriage, is clearly bizarre.

We believe that there is an urgent need for moves to help people work out their own preferred matrimonial 'code' and not to go on accepting an imposed model that, demonstrably, includes elements designed to serve the interests of dominant groups in some previous era. Some people may well wish their loving relationship to be formalised (as at present) into an all-embracing contract that is intendedly permanent, sacramental, precludes all other sexual relationships, and involves sacrifices in the woman's property rights and changes in her surname and tax position. So marriage in this form should remain as an option. But others may not wish to proceed in this way. They may wish to draw up a conjoint contract when they decide to spend their lives together. This contract would be designed to meet their current needs and to anticipate, as far as possible, future developments in their approach to, for example, joint property, sexual relationships and children. Such contracts could take a wide variety of forms according to the particular needs, hopes and expectations of the couple involved. In an age which, more than any other, places emphasis on personal growth and development as a desirable aim it seems almost foolhardy to embark on a contract at age 25 and expect it to suit one's needs for the next fifty years.

Considerable work would obviously be necessary to develop a set of suitable contracts, each readily capable of being tailored to individual needs. We suggest that here an important diversion of the energies of the legal profession could be made. At present the expensive attention of solicitors is primarily focussed on terminating failed contracts, usually in an adversarial atmosphere of bitterness and recrimination which works against the achievement of negotiated and constructive settlements. With the introduction of conjoint contracts, drawn up when the couple have strong positive feelings for each other and are highly motivated to co-operate, the solicitor's role could be much more positive. He or she might be in a good position to prevent subsequent catastrophes by helping the couple to think through the issues and agree upon the conjoint contract most suitable to them. Solicitors' wide knowledge of contract-making generally, combined with their practical experience of the pitfalls of marriage, would be invaluable for carrying out this vital preventative task. Some might object that this approach to marriage is somewhat lacking in mystery and romance. If so we can only point out that these qualities are conspicuously absent in messy divorce cases.

Whatever contracts are devised, we should wish for a recognition of the distinction between, on the one hand, the needs, rights and obligations of each partner towards the other as a contracting adult and, as a partially separate issue, their respective responsibilities and feelings towards any children. It would probably make sense for the first type of contract to be much more easily terminated than the second. The contract dealing with the children could well be embarked upon when it was decided to start a family. At this stage the partners may well be thinking more concretely about questions of child care than they were when they originally formalised their relationship. For example, their respective career prospects may be better defined. At present, in our judgment, much of the pain and suffering experienced by all those involved in a divorce is exacerbated by the conflict and confusion between the feelings the couple have about each other and the feelings they each have about the children. If the distinction between each adult as a member of a pair and each adult as a parent were to be contractually recognised (with all the thinking out this would have entailed), it might help them to sort out, following a breakdown, the negative feelings towards the partner from the positive feelings they probably both have towards the children. These latter feelings are the potentially constructive element. They might possibly be built on, at some appropriate stage, to facilitate the working out of some practical arrangements enabling the 'family', in some senses, to continue although the parents are no longer a pair together and have, in all other respects, quite separate lives.

It is clear from out study that at present we are far short of achieving such aims. Many divorcees continue to act out their pain and anger through their children by fighting over custody and access arrangements. The long-term costs for the children (the next generation of parents) are likely to be enormous unless, as a society, we have the wit to find ways of encouraging both partners to continue acting as loving parents, and perhaps even as friends to each other, even when the marital relationship has irretrievably broken down. The complete withdrawal of one of the parents during the child's formative years (an outcome apparently encouraged by some statements from the judiciary) does *not* provide a suitable model of adult behaviour for children as they develop their own views about relationships.

Present matrimonial practice serves to inhibit the sort of progress we have in mind. Church marriage is often a hypocritically 'Christian' act for those not normally religious. Paradoxically, because the service itself is for some an alien or even awesome experience, the implications of this major life decision may not be given the cool and detailed consideration they would receive in the somewhat less forbidding setting of, say, a lawyer's or marriage counsellor's office. At present discussion about the implications may be confined to a brief and ritualistic chat with the vicar. The solemn insistence on the *permanence* of the arrangement precludes the commonsense consideration that a marriage, more so than other contracts, might need to be adjusted in certain ways as circumstances change. Such adjustments reflect changing needs and personal growth; they should not be occasions for reproach. At present the only way, formally, to adjust a marriage is to end it. If more flexible arrangements meant that friendship could more often survive the ending of a marriage, more children would be spared the immense emotional pain of watching their parents at war. Perhaps they would also cease to be regarded almost as pieces of land to be held in the 'custody' of one parent while 'access' to them is granted to the other by a judge with a limited vision, based largely on precedent, of the total range of possible arrangements.

It may be argued that all this flexibility already exists. Many couples have voted with their feet by avoiding both church and registry office altogether. But at present there is no available 'model agreement' that can encourage them to think through and define their relationship to any joint property or to the future care of any children. Similarly couples, having formally assented to a marital code that precludes extra-matrimonial affairs, often find this unrealistic and may work out their own solution in this respect. But the so-called 'ideal' norms concerning sexual behaviour have been powerfully impressed upon many of us as we grew up and to depart from them can lead to considerable internal conflict which often manifests itself in the form of deception, shame or guilt. Only the most mature and resourceful individuals are therefore likely, jointly, to achieve solutions which stand outside the established norms of marriage but which, nevertheless, work well for them.

To call into question the universal appropriateness of existing matrimonial arrangements is not in the least to deny or devalue the need most people probably have to form a long-lasting, satisfying relationship with one other person. Nor do we argue that more flexible and sensitive arrangements for formalising such relationships will obviate all the misery and strain when things go wrong. Nothing could do that. But we *do* feel that the doctrines, law and expectations currently surrounding the making and breaking of marriages have finally been shown, in the last decade, to be quite unsatisfactory for many and crippling for some. The resultant carnage suffered by many of the men in this book, and the millions of others they represent, is unacceptably and unnecessarily severe. Given, too, that a main aim of marriage is the procreation and care of children, it seems evident that in this respect also the present arrangements have become sadly deficient. We feel it would be quite pointless to seek to redress this situation by exhorting people to conform more closely to a set of outdated 'rules'. It would make better sense to reform the institution so as to make it more sensitive to the diverse and changing needs of people.

Appendix 1
The Survey

Our research aim was to find out as much as possible within given constraints of time and cost, about the ways in which men experienced a divorce. Of the various research methods considered ('in depth' interviews, interviewer completed questionnaires, etc.) it was decided to base the research on a self-completed postal questionnaire. This mode of enquiry enables a broad range of questions to be asked, allows the respondent to answer in his own time without such embarrassment as might be caused by the presence of an interviewer, permits complete anonymity and is relatively inexpensive. The questionnaire form included forty-seven questions, some offering a range of answers from which one was to be chosen, others providing a space for comment on the less cut and dried issues. Answers to the latter type of question varied enormously in length from the very terse to the very discursive depending partly upon the respondent's facility with words—although there were some extremely expressive one-liners.

It was decided to supplement the findings from the questionnaires with a small number of interviews. Respondents were therefore invited to add their name and address should they be prepared to be interviewed. Over half the sample did so and of these ten were interviewed. The aim of the interviews was to gain a better insight into some of the issues that could not be adequately covered in an impersonal questionnaire and the interviewees were selected with this criterion in mind.

The selection of the main sample presented a number of difficulties. The original intention was to contact a random sample of men who had been divorced in the various courts in Sussex over the previous ten years. We hoped to enlist the co-operation of the courts and to have the letter and form forwarded by them to every n^{th} man divorced over this period (where n was calculated so as to give us the requisite total of 100). Unfortunately, despite the active interest and helpful co-operation offered at senior levels in the probation service locally, it was apparent that approval at other levels (from the local court welfare officers to the Lord Chancellor's Department) would be necessary for our material to be forwarded to a sample of divorced men by the courts. It soon became clear that this approval would not be forthcoming from every welfare officer and that the task of convincing the Lord Chancellors' Department of the significance of the study would be a lengthy one.

In the circumstances we were obliged to opt for the second best strategy of advertising the study by as many different means as possible, to send out forms when contacted by divorced men, and to call a halt when we had received 100 forms (or very nearly this member). This was clearly a rough and ready sampling procedure but we felt that if a wide variety of media were used, the form would reach a good cross-section of men. The following were among the advertising methods used:

— advertisements in the local press;
— an advertisement in the Brighton and Hove Albion Football Club programme;
— broadcasts on Capital Radio and Radio Brighton;
— a broadsheet on the notice boards of various local organisations such as sports clubs, large employers, Lewes Prison, the county police headquarters and the local social service department headquarters and area officers;
— word of mouth advertising via local clergymen, doctors, etc;
— a limited number of forms sent to Families Need Fathers and the Campaign for Justice in Divorce.

This procedure produced a total of 100 completed forms over the period March to July 1981. Of these, eight were from men who were awaiting the finalisation of their divorce and it was decided not to use these in the analysis. This book is therefore based on the experiences and comments of the remaining ninety-two men.

The ninety-two were grouped into the six occupational class divisions used by the Registrar General when drawing up census statistics:

Class I	— professional (doctors, lawyers, etc.)
Class II	— intermediate non-manual (teachers, managers, social workers, etc.)
Class III NM	— junior non-manual workers (clerks, typists, etc.)

Class III M	— skilled manual workers (toolmakers, drivers, etc.)
Class IV	— partly skilled manual workers (caretakers, storekeepers, etc.)
Class V	— unskilled manual workers (cleaners, etc.).

It is stressed that this scheme is used only because it is generally accepted in social scientific research and it enables convenient comparison to be made with other research findings. The scheme is clearly defective and reflects outdated attitudes in its implicit grouping of highly skilled and experienced manual workers on the same hierarchical 'rung' as the most junior clerical worker.

The occupational structure of the survey sample, together with the national structure, is shown in the table below.

| | | | Survey sample | National (1980—estimated) |
				(percentages)
Class	I		13.0	5.6
Class	II		38.0	26.3
		III NM	18.4	11.2
		III M	21.7	37.5
		IV	7.8	14.9
		V	1.1	4.5
			100.0	100.0

Notes:
1 The three retired men in the sample have been categorised according to their previous occupation.
2 The ten unemployed men have been categorised according to their last occupation.
3 The 1980 national figures are based on a preliminary report of the 1980 General Household Survey (see *OPCS Monitor*, 16 June 1981). As anticipated, there was a marked under-representation of manual workers in the study sample. Despite considerable effort during the latter stages of the survey period we were unable to achieve a better occupational balance.

In age, the men responding ranged from 27 to 75 at the survey date. The distribution of ages was as shown on the next page:

	Age at survey date	Age at marriage	Age at divorce
15-19		5	
20-24		28	
25-29	6	41	14
30-34	17	13	23
35-39	23	3	24
40-44	18	2	18
45-49	12		5
50-54	7		5
55-59	4		1
60-64	2		-
65-69	1		2
70-74	1		
Over 74	1		
	92	92	92

The average age at the survey date was 41 years 5 months. The average age at which the marriages had occurred was just over 26 years and the divorces had occurred at an average age of 37½.

Because of the range of advertising media used, the men in the sample were drawn from a number of counties in the south of England and some from Wales. The pattern of residential location was as follows:

	Number of men
Sussex	32
London	21
Avon	8
Wales	7
Surrey	6
Wiltshire	6
Hertfordshire	3
Kent	3
Essex	2
Oxfordshire	1
Shropshire	1
Buckinghamshire	1
Northamptonshire	1
	92

We did not feel that any significant variations in the material we were studying was likely to occur by county so the size of the area from which the sample was drawn seemed of little significance.

From the viewpoint of strictly scientific methodology, the survey procedure has two defects. The sample was not drawn in a random fashion but depended on self-selection and self-motivation to complete and send back the form. We have no precise means of knowing the non-response rate (although we know that approximately 250 forms were distributed by one means or another), nor have we any information about the differences between the group who completed the form and those who received one but opted not to complete it. It is, however, reasonable to speculate that those who did complete the form felt more strongly, positively or negatively, about their experience than those who did not. The second defect lies in the lack of any comparisons with a 'control' group of men—that is to say, a group similar in all respects to the group analysed save that they were not divorced. Both these defects were, of course, accepted from the beginning since the overall intention was to write the book in order to open up discussion of the issues rather than to produce a scientific treatise. Nevertheless we regret, in view of the obvious significance of research in this field, that more co-operation was not obtainable from the local court welfare officers or from the Lord Chancellors Department and that we were obliged to fall back onto second best measures in constructing the sample.

Appendix 2
A Method to Assess Helpfulness

In Chapter 5 we reported on the levels of help received from a variety of people and agencies. The findings were based on the following question on the survey form: *'Around the time of the break-up, did you turn to any of the following for help or advice? If so, how helpful were they?'* We listed all the possible sources of help discussed in Chapter 5 and left a space for 'Other'. Against each source we listed six possible levels of helpfulness as follows:

> Extremely helpful
> Very helpful
> Fairly helpful
> No help
> Definitely unhelpful
> Not approached.

From the responses we aimed to assess: (a) what proportion of the ninety-two men approached each source; and (b) how helpful that source had apparently been. There was no problem in calculating (a), but (b) is clearly more complex. In order to take account of the *degree* of helpfulness experienced we devised a simple arithmetic scoring system.

Response	Score
Extremely helpful	+ 3
Very helpful	+ 2
Fairly helpful	+ 1
No help	0
Definitely unhelpful	− 1

An example should make the method clear. Assume that a particular source (say, 'joint friends') had been approached by sixty-three men. Ten had found it 'extremely helpful', sixteen had found it 'very helpful', fourteen had found it 'fairly helpful', eighteen had found it 'no help' and five had found it 'definitely unhelpful'. The final score would be:

			(extremely helpful)	=	30
	10 ×	3	(extremely helpful)	=	30
	16 ×	2	(very helpful)	=	32
	14 ×	1	(fairly helpful)	=	14
	18 ×	0	(no help)	=	0

$$$$

					76
less	5 ×	−1	(definitely unhelpful)	=	− 5
	63				71

The final step was to divide this total (71) by the number of men approaching this source (63) in order to arrive at an average 'helping score' of 1.13. As shown in Chapter 5, the highest score arrived at was 1.76, the lowest was 0.06, and the average of all scores was 1.03.

Bibliography

All Party Divorce Law Reform Group, *Memorandum Presented to the President of the Family Division of the High Court*, 1980.

Anderson, M., *Approaches to the History of the Western Family 1500–1914*, Economic History Society, 1980.

Anderson, M. (ed.), *Sociology of the Family*, Penguin, 1971.

Ariès, P., *Centuries of Childhood*, Cape, 1962.

Bannister, D. and Fransella, F., *Inquiring Man*, Penguin, 1971.

Bell, C., *Middle Class Families*, Routledge, 1969.

Bellman, H., *The Silent Revolution*, Methuen, 1928.

Boggs, C., *Gramsci's Marxism*, Pluto, 1976.

Boom, B. L., White, S. W. and Asher, S. J., 'Marital disruption as a stressful life event' in *Divorce and Separation* ed. G. Levinger and C. Moles, Basic Books, 1979.

Bowskill, D., *Single Parents*, Futura, 1980.

Central Statistical Office, *Social Trends, 12, 1982*, HMSO, 1981.

Chesser, E., *Love and Marriage*, Pan, 1957.

Chester, R., 'Health and marriage breakdown: experience of a sample of divorced women', *British Journal of Preventative Social Medicine*, 25, 1971.

Church of England, *Marriage, Divorce and the Church*, SPCK, 1971.

Church of England, *Alternative Service Book*, Cambridge University Press, 1980.

Coogler, O. J., Webber, R. E. and McHenry, P. C., 'Divorce mediation— means of facilitating divorce and adjustment', *Family co-ordinator*, 28, 1979.

Cooper, D., *The Death of the Family*, Penguin, 1971.

Coser, R. L., *The Family: Its Structure and Functions*, Macmillan, 1964.

de Beauvoir, S., *The Second Sex*, Cape, 1953.

Denning Committee, *Matrimonial Causes*, Final Report, Cmd. 7024, HMSO, 1947.

Derrett, J. D. M., *Law in the New Testament*, Darton, 1970.

Dominian, J., *Marital Breakdown*, Penguin, 1968.

Drummond, M., *How to Survive as a Second Wife*, Robson Books, 1981.

Engels, F., *The Origin of the Family, Private Property and the State*, 1884.

Engels, F., *The Condition of the Working Class in England*, Panther Books, 1969.

English Law Commission, *Reform of the Grounds of Divorce: the Field of*

Choice, Cmnd. 3123., 1966.

English Law Commission, *The Financial Consequences of Divorce—Discussion Paper* No. 103, Cmnd. 8041, HMSO, 1980.

English Law Commission, *The Financial Consequences of Divorce* No. 112, HMSO, 1981.

Finer Committee, *Report of the Committee on One Parent Families*, Cmnd. 5629, HMSO, 1974.

Firestone, S., *The Dialectic of Sex*, The Women's Press, 1979.

Fletcher, R., *The Family and Marriage*, Penguin, 1962.

Goode, W. J., *World Revolution and Family Patterns*, Free Press, 1963.

Goode, W. J., *The Family*, Prentice Hall, 1964.

Gorer, G., *Sex and Marriage in England Today*, Nelson, 1971.

Grad, J. and Sainsbury, P., 'Evaluating the community psychiatric service in Chichester', *Milbank Memorial Fund Quarterly*, 44, 1966.

Grant, M., *Saint Paul*, Weidenfeld and Nicolson, 1976.

Greer, G., *The Female Eunuch*, Paladin, 1971.

Habermas, J., *Legitimation Crisis*, Heinemann, 1976.

Harris, C. C., *The Family*, Allen and Unwin, 1969.

Herbert, A. P., *The Ayes Have it*, Methuen, 1937.

Holmes, T. H. and Rahe, R. H., 'The social readjustment rating scale', *Journal of Psychosomatic Research*, 11, 1967.

Kitchin, S. B., *A History of Divorce*, Chapman, 1912.

Kuhn, A. and Wolpe, A. M., (eds.), *Feminism and Materialism*, Routledge, 1978.

Laing, R. D., *The Politics of Experience*, Penguin, 1967.

Laing, R. D., *The Politics of the Family*, Tavistock, 1971.

Laing, R. D. and Esterson, A., *Sanity, Madness and the Family*, Tavistock, 1964.

Leete, R., *Changing Patterns of Family Formation and Dissolution*, Studies on Medical and Population Subjects No. 39, HMSO, 1979.

Macaulay, M., *The Art of Marriage*, Penguin, 1957.

Mace, D. R., *Marriage*, Hodder and Stoughton, 1952.

Marx, K., *Capital*, Volume 1, Penguin, 1976.

Mayer, J. E. and Timms, N., *The Client Speaks*, Routledge, 1970.

McGregor, O. R., *Divorce in England*, Heinemann, 1957.

McMurray, L., 'Emotional stress and driving performance: the effect of divorce', *Behavioural Research in Highway Safety*, 1, 1970.

Merton, R. K. and Nisbet, R. A., *Contemporary Social Problems*, Harcourt Brace, 1971: chapter on 'Family Disorganisation' by W.J. Goode.

Millett, K., *Sexual Politics*, Doubleday, 1970.

Mitchell, J., *Psychoanalysis and Feminism*, Allen Lane, 1974.

Montefiore, H., 'Jesus on divorce and remarriage', in *Marriage, Divorce and the Church*, SPCK, 1971.

Morgan, D. H. J., *Social Theory and the Family*, Routledge, 1975.

Mortimer Group, *Putting Asunder*, SPCK, 1966.

Murch, M., *Justice and Welfare in Divorce*, Sweet and Maxwell, 1980.

Murdock, G. P., *Social Structure*, Macmillan, 1949.

OPCS, *Population Trends 13*, HMSO, 1978.

Parsons, T. and Bales, R. F., *Family, Socialization and Interaction Process*, Free Press, 1955.

Poster, M., *Critical Theory of the Family*, Pluto, 1978.

Pringle, M. K., *The Needs of Children*, Anchor, 1980.

Rakusen, M., *Distribution of Matrimonial Assets on Divorce*, Butterworths, 1979.

Reich, W., *The Sexual Revolution*, Vision Press, 1951.

Schon, D. A., *Beyond the Stable State*, Penguin, 1973.

Scottish Law Commission, *Family Law Report on Aliment and Provision*, HMSO 1981.

Shorter, E., *The Making of the Modern Family*, Fontana, 1977.

Taylor, B., *Eve and the New Jerusalem*, Virago, forthcoming 1983.

Tomalin, C. *The Life and Death of Mary Wollstonecraft*, Pelican, 1977.

Tönnies, F., *Community and Association*, Routledge, 1955.

Wallerstein, J. S. and Kelly, J. B., *Surviving the Break-up*, Grant McIntyre, 1980.

Working Party on Marriage Guidance—Home Office, *Marriage Matters*, HMSO, 1979.

Wilkinson, M., Children and Divorce, Blackwell, 1981.

Wylie, O. P., *Tax Digest, 9, Taxation on Divorce and Separation*, Winter, 1981/82.

Young, M. and Willmott, P., The Symmetrical Family, Routledge, 1973.

i

Index